BORN GAY

Mom should have known when...

BORN GAY

Mom should have known when...

recollections of childhood memories
compiled by Michael Zambotti

illustrations by Frisch

Alamo Square Press

Library of Congress Catalog Card Number: 98-073807

ISBN: 1-886360-06-5

10   9   8   7   6   5   4   3   2   1

Acknowledgments

Special thanks to Scott Meyers for his tireless dedication to assisting in typing, transcribing and word processing. Also to my mother and father who tried to understand and love me. Also, I would like to thank Jim Sandberg, Wayne Adams, Jose O., Fran S., Lynn, Doug, Bill E., Nui, R.G., Scott M., Chris M., David, Patricia Sellars, Frank, Phil & Mark, Yunor & Bill, all of my friends and the people I have met creating this book.

Introduction

I was motivated to write this book in response to the unenlightened ideas of the 1992 Republican Convention, which proposed being gay was a choice individuals made. I set out to uncover through interviews whether there were early tell-tale signs of gay behavior.

The comic stories in this book may seem frivolous but together they make an important point: gay young people show distinctive behavior patterns from very early on. These patterns emerged as I interviewed hundreds of gay men about their childhood experiences.

Being gay is a trait inborn at birth, not a choice. It is much the same as being born short or tall, right or left-handed, intelligent or dull. A gay child often knows he is different very early and gropes for ways to identify, to understand, to experience the nature of his differences. It is an unfair society that discriminates against people for following their own nature, or worse yet forces them to repress their true nature in order to fit in and be accepted.

Gay children and teenagers exist, require understanding and in many cases protection by their parents, and sometimes from them, as well as protection in the schools. Sadly, hundreds of gay and lesbian teenagers opt for suicide each year, rather than subsist in a living hell of maltreatment by family, schoolmates and even teachers. Gay youngsters are harassed, ridiculed and even physically attacked because they are different.

This book may give parents clues to whether their sons are gay and hopefully lead them to give their gay sons the necessary love and support to be successful at being themselves and fulfilling their own potential. Thousands of successful gay men and lesbians today offer witness that living gay can be a rewarding lifestyle for those who are born with this propensity and learn to respect themselves as they are.

Of course, the book can also be read for the sheer joy of sharing childhood memories. For gay men and lesbians these stories will illicit nostalgic recollections of their own quests for wholeness.

Over a period of years, during which time I lived in Italy, Czech Republic, Germany, New York, California, Hawaii, Australia, Holland and Pennsylvania, I collected these stories. More came in through the information super highway. The men that I interviewed were from every occupation imaginable, from all 50 states and over 31 countries. Over a third of the men questioned did not have stories.

I had no idea what kind of stories I would uncover, and I was surprised so many of them involved drag and women's clothes. It is likely that young gay men are grasping to understand the liminal state between maleness and femaleness, and gender in our culture is largely defined by apparel. Our culture also finds cross-dressing amusing and many of these stories are remembered because they were viewed as comical and vividly reinforced by the reactions and memories of family members and friends.

The varying reaction of the parents is significant. Parents are sometimes hostile and angry, sometimes loving and understanding.

How it all relates to the socio-economic class structure adds an extra dimension. It seems that the men who most successfully deal with their sexuality are from families where the individual child is supported and encouraged to be who he is, not what the parents wish him to be. In such families, children are given opportunities to pursue their own personal best, as in sports and the arts, and women are treated with respect and equality. The more macho and aggressive, competitive and anti-feminine the family and subculture, the more gay boys seem likely to dress in drag or generally behave bizarrely.

Children experiment with sex. This is a fact and in this book you will find an array of different ways that gay male children act out their fantasies. It is unfair to pass judgment on anyone, especially children desperately seeking their sexual identity. As I listened to stories of child abuse, incest, violence and experimentation, all told with candor and pride of survival, it gave me hope. I hope you react that way as well.

Mike Zambotti
Los Angeles, CA
September, 1998

BORN GAY

Mom should have known when...

I was nine years old and my father was a professor at the United States Air Force Academy in Colorado Springs, Colorado. He used to take me to the gym with him and we would walk through the locker room. I remember seeing all of those naked cadets. I was so excited my heart was pounding so hard I thought it was going to explode. Even then, I sadly realized that I must not get found out or I would be in trouble. I knew I had to hide these feelings.

Cyril

Two punk rock stars would often come to our house dressed in leather; one was a woman with huge boobs and the other was a guy. I was six at that time. When they visited the house, my father would want me to run and hug her and I would, for a second, and then I would hug the male rocker and get a boner. I didn't know why. My mother was embarrassed that I was bothering the guy all night.

Michelangelo, Italy

My friend Steve and I would watch *Scoobi Doobi Doo*, the TV show, we both thought that the blond cartoon character Darren was so sexy, so hot. We were only seven at the time. We never thought it odd that we found a guy attractive, but looking back it was a clue.

Matthew

Friday nights I used to love to sit with my mother and watch Tom Jones. She would be staring at his hairy chest and so would I.

Ken

When I was ten, I saw the inside cover of Grand Funk Railroad album. I couldn't stop thinking about it, I just was so interested and wanted to be in a room with these naked men. I didn't have defined thoughts, I just had a feeling. When I was ten, I looked at teeny-bopper magazines, staring for hours at photos of David Cassidy and Bobby Sherman.

Clifford

I had no idea of sexual dichotomies in the fifth grade; all I knew was that I got hot and cold sensations being around a boy named Steve. We were as close as friends could be; swapping homework, and spending weekends at each others homes. Stevie had two very cute sisters, twins a year older. My family and other friends just presumed I had a crush on Michelle and Sandy. I liked playing with Sandy, but my concentration was on Stevie. One night I was rubbing a fingernail up and down his back, butt and legs. I then started licking him and suddenly his hard weenie was in my mouth. No coming. But long kissing and giggling before we fell asleep. Next morning I saw Sandy changing clothes. To be "nasty" I took her panties. They smelled funny, but nice, just like Steve's underwear. My sister found the panties and that got me a "facts-of-life" lecture and sermon. My heart broke the next year when a pretty new girl enrolled in sixth grade and every boy was gaga over her, including Steve. I was inconsolable. Everybody thought I was sad over Sandy, now in Junior High, finding a beau. Luckily, because these two events happened at the same time, no one caught on. Dumb or innocent, I was spared compound anxieties.

Steve and I did not have heavy sex until senior grade. I developed into a gay fantasist, thinking of the football team showering before I went to bed. But I had a girlfriend, whose best friend started dating Steve. When she dumped him, I offered comfort in an impromptu whirl of anal sex and long 69-ing. It was friend-lust that had a special magic. Later he demanded I drop my girlfriend and not see any other guys and that I attend to him. My indecision led him into

10

the arms of a big college jock. Such ironies, when he outed himself, he did so with a vengeance and I just allowed bisexuality to be my way in bed. No belated shocks from the folks.

The strangest thing and an interesting epilogue is that at our tenth high school reunion, I went with a casual male lover and Stevie was with Tenny, the high school cheerleader who soured him on women. She went home with an old teacher, my date took off to an all night J/O bachelor party. Steve and I are now talking about a closet marriage. We are back together.

Stanley

I used to play Mystery Men when I was five or six. It was a board game with little doors and there were all these men on cards and one would be on the door and you would pick one. I knew which man I wanted. I played this game with all the girls, you also picked what dress you wanted to wear. It's a little girls game. I thought it was great. It was daring if you chose the mustached man, because he was considered sexy, wild and *bad*.

Elliot

I was nine or ten when I cut up my mother's favorite material to make dresses for my sister's Barbies. My mom was so mad at me she yelled and screamed. To this day she tries to make me feel guilty about it. That should have been a clue. I was the last one playing Barbies after my sisters got bored. Hours later I was still going strong with the dream house and the pink jeep and Barbie's clothes. My mom and dad walked by and saw me and just kind of shook their heads. It was the classic Barbie thing. I spent a lot of time with Barbie. I had a carrying case. It was square with a handle. It was that shiny pink vinyl material, and I kept my GI Joe in there, but I also kept Barbie and Ken. And I had little pink hangers, and I would hang my GI Joe clothes on the hangers in the little Barbie doll case. My grandmother gave it to me.

Ken

When I was three, I remember living with my parents in a very old house. There was a bathroom with a shower, but the bathtub was in the cellar. I was in the bath with my father, looking at his dick and balls. I reached up and pulled myself up by his dick and he hit me.

When I was six years old and had a dream about my teacher. I was naked with him in bed and we were hugging and he was lying on me. It was nice. I woke up afterwards and I was totally wet. Not wet with ejaculation, of course: I was six—it was pee.

My first contact was with a playmate at 11. I was in his bedroom and we talked and he was sitting on a chair, backwards with his legs spread. He had a big bulge and we talked about sex (that's normal at that age) and we talked about girls, but inside I hoped there would be more. He was totally hard and we sucked and that was it. Afterwards, I phoned him every day to have him help me with my math. He came over, but we didn't do mathematics.

Henri, Belgium

When I was about 14 years old, I used to go over to my best friend's house. I was so in love with his brother, I would go over and fantasize about his riding me on his motorcycle. He would sit in front and I was holding him around his waist. We would ride up and down the hills and everything. I used to fantasize about grabbing his crotch. I got the nerve and was going to do it but I never ever did it, but it still brings me to an incredible orgasm. In 1981, I was 12 and 1981 Roller Disco King of Florence, Alabama.

Billy

I had a crush at five on a guy in the Michigan State Toy Box Theater. He was cute in tights as the Pied Piper of Hamlin Town in the show.

At 16 years old, my father walked into the living room at 3 am and I had stolen one of the dining room candle sticks and it was up my butt. I was masturbating when he caught me. What a scene! Try to explain your way out of that.

Kelvin

12

In high school in my teens, I had the crush on this guy. He was my perfect type, so I made sure that I was his friend. For a couple years we were inseparable. One night we went to the house of an older friend out in the country. This older guy lived in a trailer. Now this was Atlanta, and we all got really drunk that night, just completely drunk. And when it came time to go to bed, he and my buddy and I ended up in the same bed by some miracle, who knows. Somehow we were laying there and we started playing with each other. I was really excited, but after five minutes, he just passed out. He was passed out, but he had this rock-hard giant cock. So I just went over there and put my mouth on it and started sucking his cock. I was having a great time, 'cause this was my fantasy, you know, come true. And basically that's the story and then I came all over the place. He didn't. He was passed out. (Is this when you believed in God for the first time?) Yeah, I think so.

Ned

I work in a German preschool, kindergarten, and sometimes the parents come in and say, "What's wrong with our child? He always plays with the girls and he's doing this and that." And the teachers and I, we just tell the parents right out, we say, "Your son is a homosexual. He's gay." And sometimes they're really upset and they cry and other times they just accept it. But in Germany here, we are much more open and we just tell them. In every class there are a couple of boys that are different and a few girls that just want to play with the boys and do rough things.

Deitrich

As a child I had girls instead of boys for friends; I had trouble mixing with the straight boys. Children at that age know it somehow. Sometimes they would tease me at the worst moment. Sometimes the boys would invite me to fun gatherings, because I would be the clown, but never on the camping trips.

Jonathan, Germany

13

Every year we'd go see *Holiday on Ice* when it came to the Memorial Auditorium in Chattanooga, Tennessee. Afterwards I would spend a couple of weeks copying the skating outfits out of the souvenir programs with pen and crayons to make paper dolls. This probably went on about six years—by then, I was 15. I still have those programs.

Gerald

Around the age of eight to ten, I would play with the girl across the street and we would play with her Barbies and parade around in her mother's taffeta ball gowns.

By the age 11, I had a collection of troll dolls with the troll house and everything; I would spend hours in the bathroom setting and styling their hair. When they looked their best, I would stage beauty pageants.

Age six, I insisted on dressing as a witch on Halloween in a costume my mother made for me (The first in a long line of drag experiences). How I convinced my conservative mother to make me a dress is beyond me.

14

I wanted to study ballet; so when I was seven or eight, I started classes and performed in the Nutcracker Suite in San Francisco until my father decided it wasn't a good idea. When I wore my tights around the house that was the last straw for my father

When it was time to choose a musical instrument, I wanted to play the harp, but my parents would not let me, so I settled on the violin.

I practiced gymnastics with the girls in the neighborhood and could do the Chinese splits at age 12.

I showed a precocious interest in interior design. I furnished my room with a harvest-gold shag bedspread, avocado sculptured wall-to-wall carpeting, rust and avocado custom-made draperies, in what I thought was the height of fashion. This was Concord, California in the early 1970s.

I idolized Julie Andrews and I would sing just like her. Until my voice changed at 13. By 15, my perfect soprano voice was lost forever.

Hermie

I'm a psychiatrist and my friend is a psychiatrist with a three-year-old son; she's pretty sure he's going to be gay because... Well, she has two sons. The oldest one is five. And he's all boy. He's rambunctious and hyperactive and he plays with swords and guns and all the rest. Her younger son is three and he's extremely sweet, loving, easy to get along with, eager to please her. One day they are shopping for shoes, walking around the boys section. And the older one is grabbing all these Mutant Ninja Turtle shoes to try on, and they couldn't find Daniel, the younger one. So they go looking for him and he's strolled off into the little girls section and he's picking up these little pink slippers and wanting to put them on. And they said, "No, no, no. We have to go to the boy's section." And he just refused and said he just wanted to try on these pink shoes. So they're pretty sure he's gay, but they're cool about it.

Hugh

15

At the age of three, I went through a stage where I gave myself a new name every day; after the first few days, I switched from boy names to girl names.

At the age of nine or ten, when my cub scout group decided to put on a skit about the circus, all the other boys wanted to be costumed as clowns, acrobats, lion tamers and ringmasters, but I dressed up as the circus fat lady.

Jonathan

I can remember my parents wondering what they were going to do with me because I wouldn't wear regular Levi jeans. I had to wear Levi corduroy jeans in the different colors. They would sit up at night worrying about why I wouldn't wear these pants and I had to have a certain kind. They just didn't know what to do with me. They were at their wit's end.

Gregory

My sister should have figured out that I was gay when I was 18 and I always made sure that her hat, belt, purse and pumps matched. We used to go shopping together and I made sure she looked flawless.

I begged for tap dancing lessons when I was 12 years old. I used to put Desitin ointment on my butthole, the diaper rash stuff. I really did. I was five years old. I rolled up toilet paper and put it in my underwear, like Kotex. I don't know why. I guess that maybe I saw my mom doing it. I remember my mother's silver, thigh-high go-go boots. They were fabulous. I was so pissed when she cut them off at the end of the '70s.

In elementary school, the girls used to ask you to look at your fingernails. If you stuck your hand out flat and looked at them that way, you were gay. And if you curled your hand in and looked at them that way, you were straight.

The Marlboro man got me excited. I just remember the back cover of a magazine and I was eight. I gave my first blow job at age eight to the baby-sitter. Also, I cried at "The Grinch who Stole Christ-

16

mas" and none of my seven brothers cried, just me.

I seduced the senior class president when I was a sophomore. With my brothers I used to always have to play the wife when we would play games. When I was ten, I tried on my neighbors prom dress. No one knew, no one saw me. I was very discrete about it. My mom was devastated when she determined that I was gay. I was born in Salt Lake City: Mormon. I loved to wear high heels. I was a gymnast and a cheerleader. What more could they want?

Fred

I spent, every second of Christmas morning, when I was ten years old, with my sister's Barbie dolls. More time than she did. The whole morning and probably weeks after that, dressing them, playing with them; that damn pink Corvette was the best damn thing I ever had. Mom and Dad were pretty okay with it, I guess. I don't know.

I didn't start experimenting with gay sex until I was in college at 20, so they wouldn't have caught me physically. They didn't know through high school because I didn't give any clue, I dated girls and stuff like that. But if they had seen me in college, definitely, they would have caught on. In college, I started dating guys, and it's been all down hill from there. Thank you for dredging up the memories, damn you.

Nathan

We're talking about a...a friend of mine. Not me. This friend, he was quite a queen and looked like Elizabeth Taylor when he did drag. All he had to do was put some lipstick on and he looked great. So his mother should have known. He was about 25 years old. And his mother, you won't believe this, I don't know for what reason, she was going through his bags and she found a dildo. And she sort of confronted him with it and said, "What do you do with this?" And he said, "Mom, I stick that up my ass while I jerk off." She should have known then.

William

17

I was ten years old and I was dressed in my mother's dress and shoes when she wasn't home. I'm a big klutz and fell down the entire flight of stairs, landed in this mess at the bottom, just as they were walking in the door: a clump of dress, heels, accessories and makeup. Two years ago at a Halloween party, I looked fabulous in a black sequined dress and managed to fall down a large staircase to the amazement of the entire gathering and landed in a rumpled mess at the bottom, once again.

Tom

My mother does know, but she doesn't want to say anything, because if I'm not, she doesn't want to hurt my feelings. I'm 17 and I live in San Clemente. I dress in my sisters' clothes; I look better than she does in them. And my sisters have gotten bitter. My sister's a lesbian and my mother should have known she was a lesbian when she bought a motorcycle. My mother told me she was in love with her college roommate for two years. She said no matter what I am, whatever I do, she'll be so proud of me.

Dwayne

I was at a huge 25th wedding anniversary of someone in my family, like my aunt. I was seven. The party was in the basement and some of the older kids put me in a ballerina outfit upstairs and shoved me down the stairs in front of every one. So I made this grand entrance down the stairs in front of my extended family wearing this ballerina outfit.

Maurice

I've got a story for you. First grade and I was playing with my best friend Emily. We went back to my family's house, and we decided we were going to dress up. And I think I first put on my dad's shoes and his shirt and everything, and she put on some of my mom's clothes. And then we both kind of got this idea, and we dressed me up in my mom's clothes, too. And I had her high heels on and her shirt, and we put on makeup and all this stuff. And then the bedroom door opened and in walked my mom and there I was all dressed up in drag at six years old. She didn't know what to think. She kind of laughed and made me take the clothes off and everything. She didn't punish me. I think she thought it was funny at the same time. We still laugh about it. Had she told my dad, he would have freaked out. I'm an only child. My whole family knows about my lifestyle. My mom is very accepting, but my dad really isn't at all. They're divorced now. My mom's cool. We still joke about it and stuff.

Eric

When I wore the dress that my mom wore to her sorority pledge party and her cha-cha heels, it was fabulous; I was fabulous. I would have been about ten years old. The dress was green and big and wide and white, with tons of crinoline, like an old '50s number. She never saw me in it luckily. Also, I used to have slumber parties with the other boys and run around naked. We would pull on each others' things. That was always fun. All that horsing around. My father made me shower with him up until I was 13, that was great. But my therapist said that it was a little strange.

Frank

I did dress up in a dress with a neighbor girl: heels and gown; but that doesn't count though, every kid does that. I started molesting the one neighbor kid and his mother wouldn't let him come and play anymore. That was at eight. I set up a dungeon under the garage. I envisioned myself as a mad scientist. I tied him up. I laughed like a bad actor as he struggled against the restraints and asked to be let free. Eventually, I let him free because he wasn't having fun and that spoiled it for me. I must have been a tortured kid to do that. My brother had sex with me. I was eight, he was 11. He called it "making a bridge" and he would grind into me. At 17, I was arrested in a public restroom at the beach.

Martin, 67

19

I used to have all my little friends over and I would suck them off when I was five. Years later when I told my mom I was gay and this story from my childhood, she said that she should have known when she had noticed that all the little boys who came to visit always left with their zippers down.

Austin

I coerced my cousin into having sex with me at about age nine, I guess, into giving me a blow job. I told him it would be fun and something he should try, you know, and it was all right. And then, the things we did together sort of progressed. Eventually, as we got older, it didn't really appeal to him, because he was straight deep down. Nevertheless we jacked off together and that sort of thing.

Phil

I remember one Christmas in 1962 when I was seven years old. Being half Italian, Christmas was always a big family affair and I remember how all my male cousins on this Christmas morning opened their gifts of cowboy and Indian sets, cap guns, and all! I got exactly what I'd asked Father Christmas for that year, which was toy cooker—like a range—and it was complete with pans and a recipe book!! I spent all that Christmas day pretending to cook for my favorite uncle (who had very hairy legs I remember) and when I'd finished playing with the cooker I rolled his trouser leg up and stroked his leg while I was sitting on the floor, watching TV. I promise you that every word of this is true. I was 23 years of age when my poor mother asked me, "Darling are you a homosexual?" She was still quite shocked when I replied, "Yes Mother, I am. How did you guess?" She took it very well I am glad to say!!!!!!!!

Orsin, London

I had an Easy-Bake Oven, but I don't associate that fact with the fact that I was gay until later. I was five at the time. I always sat by the cute boys in the new home room each year.

It isn't a choice. I know that for sure. I guess Mom suspected all the time. She knows now after 40 years. I never sat down and said, "Mom, I'm gay." But she knows. I fooled around with all the kids in school, and my cousins at six or seven.

Chas

At Halloween, I put curlers in my hair. I had pretty blond hair with a blue dress, and I was so cute. And I went to the door of the neighbor who knew me very well and the neighbor lady said to her husband, "Honey, come see this little girl dressed like Dolly Parton." She didn't recognize me at all. I said, "I'm a boy dressed like a girl." And I raised my dress to show her and ran. I'm still lifting my skirt even today, but I don't do drag.

Todd

I was nine, in the shoe store with my mom. While she was busy, I tried on these display shoes: brown plastic, spiked slip-on pumps. They fit perfectly. So then, she actually bought them for me. I was nine. I wore them everywhere around the house, even in the yard. One time, I was prancing in the back yard and my dad was working chopping wood and he got mad at me for something and he grabbed my shoes off me and he chopped off the heels. I cried and cried. But the next day I kept wearing those shoes even though they were pointing up like boats and they were clomping like Peter Fonda's boots. They were uneven. I was walking heal-toe, heal-toe in those things. But I kept wearing my pumps. This all happened in Austria.

Gerald

We were camping in the basement. We got a tent for the holidays. I set it up with my two best friends. We're in the tent, and wondered what to do now, this was kind of boring. So, we played strip poker. We're like taking off all our clothes, hanging out in the tent, and kind of like exploring or whatever. And all of a sudden, my mom knocks on the tent, just kind of hits the tent as she walks by, "Hey, how's it going in there?" And we're like "Aaargh." All of us are like completely nude. It was pretty bad. I never felt so humiliated. I'm like, "Okay, Mom's home. Let's take the tent outside." We're like 13, 14, 15. One of the guys is gay, the other is apparently straight; he has a family now, but he was the one who was most aggressive. The rest of us were just exploring.

Clarence

My mother should have known when I was playing around with Robbie Sardonia when I was age five and I told her I liked it. He was the first person I messed around with. He was also five. I told her what I did every time—that's how she knew. I told her it was fun. She wasn't shame-based about it; she didn't put me down, but she said I shouldn't do it anymore. It's great because she loves me unconditionally.

Jeffery

22

That was a long time ago for us, 40 years ago, almost 25 years for my lover here. I think maybe when I didn't ask for a football, as a child and when I asked for one of those Easy-Bake Ovens when I was eight or nine. One of those electrical jobbers with the light bulb, you used to bake cakes in. It's probably a little too young for you. Oh, God.

Jason

My neighbor and I used to play and we used to wrestle. We were 13 years old. And one day we were wrestling and I swear he ejaculated on me. He said he spit on me. I thought he had orgasmed, came on me, and I liked that. But I didn't think anything bad about it. Eventually, he moved away.

Shane

When I was 18 or 19, I had to tell my mother I was gay. My friends and I were talking about Dorothy this and Dorothy that, and so-and-so was "a friend of Dorothy." Finally, my mother said, "Dorothy, Dorothy, Dorothy, who is this Dorothy?" It was a group of gay friends and we were talking together in code and my mother overheard and we were like, "Is he a friend of Dorothy's? Is she a friend of Dorothy's? Is he a friend of Dorothy's?" And so she got wise.

Bobby

When I was 12, I was stealing the TV section of the newspaper so I could take it back to my bedroom and look at the pictures of Batman and Robin. Something about Robin in those tights, I didn't know what, but I was really attracted to him. Also, the young hot kid, Robin, running with an older, "what-I-thought" was a masculine man. Looking back they were the campiest gayest characters.

I also dressed up in my mother's clothes. I had a vacuum cleaner as a child, unbelievable but true. I wanted a vacuum cleaner and they gave me one as a birthday present. It was a pink one, it worked perfectly well, but it was for little girls.

Kent

23

When I was in fifth grade, about ten years old, I dressed up in drag for Halloween, the whole deal—wig, makeup, dress, heels, jewelry. It was fun, but not unusual, since lots of guys did drag for Halloween.

One of my favorite television shows growing up was *Batman*, and I always loved Catwoman the best. I mean, all the sexual double entendres, that tight cat-suit and everything. I liked Robin, too, but we all know the truth about Bruce Wayne's relationship with his youthful ward. But, the absolute best was Batgirl. She had that neat hidden wall in her apartment and that form-fitting, vinyl suit and the entrance to her hidden Batgirl cycle. We would sometimes pretend to be super heroes; I always wanted to be Batgirl. I also liked Wonder Woman. Gee, Mom, get a clue. I had GI Joes growing up and always hated that they were anatomically incorrect. Something has got to be done about that. They should make a Ken doll to go with the anatomically unbelievable Barbie.

Mark

I had sex with the whole neighborhood, I built a tent in the spare bedroom at eight. I would bring them in the tent; it was made of material that you could see out, but parents couldn't see in. The boys would come into the tent and I would take off their pants sometimes. I would take mine off and touch them. I was an early bloomer. I told my parents I was gay at 23. They said that they knew since I was four! I hope it was not from seeing me in that tent.

We used to go to the beach after church every Sunday in Huntington Beach, California and we would walk along the Pacific Coast Highway where the surfers parked and changed. My dad would have to slap me and tell me to stop staring at the surfers changing out of their wetsuits into their towels. I used to hope that the towel would fall. Another time I was changing in a racquetball club, and I was 12 and there was a boy there that was 20 and I always remember that he had a nice dick and a perfect pubic hair. He had gorgeous, perfect pubes and body. I will never forget that vision.

Arnold

I used to masturbate in the window of my house so people could see me, especially the construction workers who were building a house right next to mine. My shower has a window from the waist up. I would stand on a ledge so I was, well everything was exposed and I would beat off in front of these construction workers. And they would yell, "Get the hell out of here, you sicko." But some of them would watch. That's probably the ballsiest thing I ever did. Afterwards, after I came and didn't feel horny anymore I used to say to myself, "Why did I do that?" And now years later I realize that you always feel like that after you have sex and come. "Why did I do that."

Brent, 19

I went to the Cow Palace in San Francisco, to exhibit my livestock, when I was ten-12 years old and had some funny experiences. I was a farm boy from Northern California I went to the show to exhibit my dairy cows and livestock, etc. They had a Batman promotion or event one day and I insisted on watching him drive around the arena in the Batmobile. Afterwards I went up and waited in a long line to get the signature of and photo of Batman.

At nine years old, I used to watch Jack Lalane exercise shows all the time, today I work out and am in good shape.

Joel

I was born in Montebello, California. My mother's the church lady. She mails me Bible verses and tapes, and she knows I am gay. That's why she sends them. She says she wants to see me in the kingdom of heaven and I say, "I'll be there, I'll be the one with pink wings." My mom asked how it happened that I became gay. I said, "It wasn't that I was molested or anything traumatic like that. I found out in church, in a fire and brimstone sermon about homosexuality in the Lutheran church." She was floored. Hearing that sermon helped me give a name to the feelings I had. I was very young, four or five years old at the time.

Theo

25

I grew up in Malibu, California and my parents were Christian Scientists. At ten years old, I remember vividly my sister calling me a fag. I was so upset that I ran into my room and cried for hours. I knew she was right and I knew that society hated fags and that I was one. I cried hysterically and my mom came in and said that it's all right that my sister was only teasing. And then my mom asked me why I was crying so much. I knew even at that age that I could not tell them the truth. Anyway, after I stopped crying I walked out into the living room and called my sister a lesbian.

Sam

They should have figured out that I was gay, because every year when it was time to write our Christmas lists, I would go through the Sears catalogue searching. Then I would cut out major home appliances and paste them to my Christmas list, like washers, dryers, blenders, hair dryers. I would be really pissed when Christmas came and Santa would bring me like toys. It's totally true. I wanted major home appliances.

Kerry

I was majorly sexually repressed because I didn't have an orgasm until I was 17 years old. The first time I ever came I came inside my girlfriend. After we left for college, I knew it was over with her, but what was I going to do? I had never masturbated. That's when I started masturbating and making up for lost time. After I started masturbating, I realized why I had been getting erections during *My Three Sons*, *Flipper* TV shows, and gladiator movies since I was seven years old. My mother should have known I was gay when I started watching gladiator movies instead of playing sports. I was attracted to and fantasized about men.

After my 18th birthday everything started to make sense: I was gay. On my 19th birthday I had my first experience with a male model in Chicago. Usually everyone's first experience is quick and over fast but with this model it was romantic from the very first kiss.

I knew it was right. It lasted until he committed suicide while filming a movie in Greece. He was 26. He may have been murdered by the Greek models who were jealous of him because he was getting all the jobs. His photo was on all the billboards and this made the others jealous. Thus the murder may have been covered up by the police, his sister went to Greece and that's what she thought. Another weird thing is that I have a doll collection, and I am 42 years old now. Only male dolls: GI Joe, Ken, etc.

Vance

I helped my mother in the kitchen. I'm baking cakes. I'm looking for my younger sisters and brothers. I'm helping. I'm older, ten, 12 years. At the age of eight years, my mother was pregnant and my father doesn't want this child. He left. He wasn't there, wasn't at home and I had to help. For me it was like a friendship. It was not mother and son, it was a friendship. But it was not normal. I felt that my father didn't like this, a jealousy toward my mother and me. At 14, the first time I fall in love with a boy. He was 15 years old. We were going together in the same school and I have a birthday, so we have a party in my home village. It was very nice. We have no sex.

Johannes, Germany

There is a photo of me with Grandma's high heels and both her purses at age three. I never had a single date with a woman except a prom date. I have a picture of me at the house with my brother and I could barely walk. I was two but I was in my mother's shoes on the front lawn.

Caser

My mother finally had to say to me, "You can wear those old high heeled shoes, but you can't wear my good shoes," when I would go into her closet and try to wear her high-heeled shoes around the house. I was ten years old and this is a true story.

Alfred

27

Well, years ago I walked on the back of my shoes. It made me feel like I was wearing high heels. And I distinctly remember doing this after coming from the Roxy Theater in New York City where Betty Grabel was playing. This was a hundred years ago. And I was singing this song as I was walking in the street. The song was "Down Argentina Way" and I was walking on the back of my shoes. One day my mother was on the street and saw me. She said, "what are you doing?" I really don't remember what answer I gave her. I was very careful whenever I did it again, that's for sure.

Reg

My mother used to catch me masturbating all the time. Once she told my dad. He took me aside and said it was natural, but he said it wasn't natural to be doing it in front of the full length mirror all the time. In a related incident, my sister and her friend ask me why I was always standing on my tippy toes in front of the mirror in the bathroom. They had been looking under the crack at the bottom of the bathroom door and saw just my tip toes facing the mirror. I was horrified. I turned beet red.

Barton, Australia

Three months before I told her that I was gay my mom told me this story.

It was like a year after my parents were divorced and my mom was still talking about my dad constantly, the way someone who is recently divorced does. One night we were sitting on the couch talking and my mom just sort of blurts out: "When you were little, about three years old, you would always help me do the laundry while your brother and twin sister were out playing ball. And when the dryer was done you would waddle to the dryer and pull out my silk panties and rub them all over your face and body and stuff because you liked the feel of silk. One time your father caught you and said to me, 'Don't let him do that, it will make him queer.'" Listening to my Mom, I just sort of sat there and I wanted to say to her, "Well Mom it

28

did make me queer." It would have been a great way to come out to Mom, but it was three more months before I came out to her.

Bruce

I used to think about the boy next door. He was 18 and I was 12. And I used to jerk off, but I had no conscious realization that I was gay. I just imagined that he had a hairier, bigger dick, and I imagined that he did the same things in the shower that I did. I didn't feel like I was gay, I felt like I was comparing notes of our dicks in my mind when I would think of him and masturbate.

Bill

When I was four and a half years old, I was at my grandparent's house and I found the shoes of a visiting lady. I can recall walking around in her tan leather high heels all over the house.

I asked my parents if I could stay up late to watch Marlene Dietrich starring in the televised Royal Command Performance at Albert Hall, London in 1963.

Jas, London

29

1. I carried around a rag doll clown and had it in my room till I moved out of the house.
2. I collected plush dolls into my 20's.
3. I hid a gay porno magazine under my pillow and she found it when I was 18.
4. I spent nights in my brother's bed till we were teenagers (he would say he was scared of the dark and/or lonely).
5. I liked *The Sound of Music* way too much and read all of Maria Von Trapp's books by the age of 16.
6. I enjoyed going to Mass (and not just on Sunday's)—great drag.
7. I didn't like sports no matter how much I tried (I still don't care for most sports).
8. I went in drag as my mom for Halloween when I was 18 years old.

Brian

I had to go hunting; I hated it. I would pretend to have colds. I hated pulling the heads off of pheasants. I stopped at 12. I refused. I said, "beat me, whatever, I am not going hunting and killing animals." I did ranching, hunting and the whole thing. I would take guys to the ranch, get them drunk, let them pass out and give them head. My sister had a boyfriend that always tried to get my pants off. He was 15 and I was 12. I always wondered why he never did anything sexual with my sister. She was sexual with everyone else! I used to iron my money. If I got a wrinkled dollar bill I would immediately iron it to make it nice, at nine or ten. Now I am in production at Warner Brothers and I launder their money.

Samuel

I used to dye my hair when I was 12 or 13. First I bleached it, and then I went black. It was always either black or blond. The kids teased me at school, but it just encouraged me. It allowed me to be more myself, be more open with myself. It gave me an excuse to be more eccentric.

Gil

I refused to pick up a gun and my whole family's into hunting. I wouldn't bait a hook when I was a teenager. I learned Shakespeare; my friends and I would go to the pool hall and I would just watch and sit there reading the Bard and memorizing it all at the pool hall.

Alan

I was 15. I was into special effects for films, models, latex rubber. I got a whim to make a dildo or phallus with a paper towel roll and Styrofoam ball and I put ten coats of rubber on it. I would take it orally in my mouth. I had no conscious idea that this was sexual or homosexual. I just wanted to do it and I was creative, so I did it.

Howard

I wore my sister's training bra at 16. My dad caught me. I was on the bathroom floor. I had my dick in one hand and the bra strap in another and my dad walked in as I was lying on the floor masturbating. They didn't yell. They tried to encourage me. They said, "Oh, it's normal; it means nothing. It's not unusual." All boys do that. Wake up, Mom and Dad.

Dennis

My parents lived one hour away from where I lived with my lover. My lover and I were on the patio sunning naked. So I asked them to call before coming over and they did call and said they would be over in one hour. Eventually, I was having sex with my boyfriend and my parents and their friends saw us. Apparently they had rang the front door bell but we didn't hear it and they tried the door and it was open so they walked in and came through to the back of the house to the sliding glass doors and there we were going at it naked and everything. But here is the classic part, they turned around walked out the front door after they saw us and shut the door. We put our clothes on. Then they rang the door bell again. We answered the door and everyone acted like nothing happened. I was 23 at the time.

Robin

31

When my mother came into the room, she plied me for information about the sounds coming from my closet. Then she threw open the doors and found somebody hiding in there that she didn't know. It was a boy I was having sex with. I had been sleeping with him the last six months. She threw him out of the house, and I talked her into letting him come back in, because he was a homeless person and didn't have anywhere to go. He had been kicked out of his house by his parents and I gave her a big sympathy ploy. So she inevitably let him come back into the house, just for that night, of course. He would sleep in the den and I would sleep in my room and it never worked out that way, of course. I was 15. He stayed in our house for another six months with my mother's consent.

Luis

I got caught at the age of nine with another guy. I was caught by my grandfather. This is what happened: It was, like, there were a couple of my friends. There was a guy and his brother, anyway we got caught. It looked like he was socking it to me, but he wasn't. So my grandfather went in and said, "What is he doing?" And he slapped the guy and I went to bed and that was it. I was always dressing up in my grandmother's clothing which she liked because I looked like a little girl. The good news is that I overcame these traumas and became a professional figure skater.

Henry

My parents...oh my god...when my dad caught me in the hay barn with my Uncle Mike. He was 16 and I was 11. We lived on a dairy farm in Idaho. We messed around for a year and a half. My dad caught us once. I had no idea how long my dad was standing there. We didn't do anything major though.

My dad had a second chance to figure out I was gay at Boy Scouts, when this boy was playing grab ass with me. We were on a hike and he kept grabbing my butt. He was 14 and I was 16. We had to camp over night by ourselves for a wilderness merit badge—just the two of us. After setting up the tent together far from everyone else and talking for a long time, he showed me he had a hard-on while we were in the tent. I sucked him, then I looked up at his face after a bit and he had a look of panic. So, I stopped. We went to sleep without talking about it. In the morning, he was gone. He told my dad who was the scoutmaster everything when he got back to the base camp. My dad had a long talk with me. We were raised Mormon so you can imagine my father's reaction. There are like 1000 guys, queers in Salt Lake City that have a similar story, messing around in the Boy Scouts.

Devin

I told my parents that I was gay when I was 18, but they didn't believe it until I was 22. The story goes like this: I had been out on this date with this guy and I was taking him home in my parents' car and he told me to pull over behind this school. So I did and then we went and played on the playground equipment. There was like this mound of dirt between the parking lot and the playground that made it completely impossible to see from the car to the playground. While we were rolling around on the grass kissing, some cop drove by and saw my car there. He came back half an hour later and my car was still there, so he reported it as an abandoned vehicle. It was a small town so word travels fast. A few minutes later my friend and I got into my car and he was giving me a blow job and out of nowhere my parents drove up and saw my face and then his head come up out of my lap. They freaked out. They saw him like sucking my dick. Needless to say, my mother gets out of my dad's truck and says, "I want to talk to you as soon as you get home, young man." That ought to be in about 20 years.

Jack

I was watching the house when my parents were out of town, I had this sudden urge to go in my father's underwear drawer, find his jock strap and suck on it. I was 14.

Jeff

33

"HANG ON TOTO!"

My mother should have known I was gay when I was caught at the age of six behind the furnace in the basement. I was with my best friend Scott Tolanson, who was five. We were naked and playing around with each other. They ignored it. They told us to put our pants back on, that's about it. Those experiences are important, part of normal childhood behavior.

The other thing I used to do when I was about six or seven was play Oz. Three girls around my age lived next door, and they had a toy box full of dresses. When they went on vacation, their toy box was out on the front porch, and I would use their clothes to dress up in and play pretend. Mother had red high heel shoes that she used to wear, and I would wear them, in turn playing The Wizard of Oz and and Dorothy. I would fling myself around Mom's bedroom like the tornado had just hit the house, yeah, that whole scene. "There's no place like home, Auntie Em, Auntie Em."

Andre

My father caught me with a hot Latino in the bathroom when I was 17. He asked me to take my friend home, come back and have a long talk. We discussed the facts of life. He took my car away for six months. That didn't stop things at all. I was on my knees, sucking dick in the shower when he caught me. He didn't see it, thank God. I wouldn't be alive today.

There was an elementary school with a big canal in the back and there was a drive for the trucks to go by, next to the canal. One afternoon I was walking by the canal, and this gas truck came by, and the driver called me over and said, "Come on over." I was like 15 years old. The guy pulled out dirty magazines with guys and women doing it and flicked the pages in front of me. And I'm inside the cab of the truck with him, and he pulled out his dick. He had a beautiful dick and he said, "Do you want to touch it?" And I said, "Yeah." I went back a few different days to see if the guy came back. He never did. I was heart-broken.

Mike

One Halloween I dressed up as a princess and I was six and we went trick-or-treating and we went to my parents' friends who were 65 and so I was in a princess gown and rang the doorbell. They said, "Oh, you look so good," and she had no idea that I was the next door neighbor boy who she knew, and she said, "Where are your parents?" My parents were hiding in the bushes. I said, "I really want coffee. I really want cappuccino." Then my parents jumped out.

Pavel

35

My cousin taught me how to go and meet men at the bathrooms in the department store at the shopping mall. The signal was to sit in the stall and pat your foot.

Once, I went there into the stall and this guy patted his foot and he was going to get together with me, but he was a worker there. He seemed very interested in me, but he said that if I ever do it again that I would be caught and not to do it again. But I didn't believe him. A month later, I went back and did the same thing. I was sitting in the stall, patting my foot and everything went silent except this man on the walkie-talkie, he goes, "I've got one." I was sweating from head to toe, and I was like, "Oh, my God, I have to get out of here before..." And when I went out there were security people on both side of the entrance of the bathroom, they caught me. I was terrified. They took me into this office and there were seven people in there in suits, and they were saying, "why are you doing this, you know? I mean you're having sex in the bathroom of our department store." They were totally intimidating me, interrogating me. And they were going to call my mother.

I begged them and I told them the reason was that my father's gay and so am I. That's why I'm here doing this. They let me go. I went home. They never called my mother and I never went back there again. Ever. But it was the most terrifying thing in my childhood. I was 14, 15. My cousin Tim is the one who introduced it to me and told me how to do it. Of course, I mean, it aroused me, but I think that's completely natural for someone 14 years old. Even though I'm gay, it's, you know, exciting. Tim now has major problems with himself, identifying with his gay side. He tries to lead the heterosexual lifestyle, but, every time I see him it's totally wrong. I think he has a drinking problem.

Michael

I was having sex with my twin from the age of six or seven, until we were freshmen in high school. There were probably four or five other guys and we were all fooling around by age eight. My mother always thought something was going on, but I had locks on my doors. We had 30 acres of land and my mother would look for us and we'd be up in the barn or up in the trees doing something with other guys.

My mother caught us all once. She came to the barn and said, "What's going on?" And we were all putting our clothes on. Eight guys. So she knew something was up, but she didn't do anything. My brother's a fireman now, and he's not straight. My mother couldn't stand this one kid who was very effeminate; he used to put flowers in his hair. And he'd take a blanket and wrap it as a sarong. My mother realized something was wrong with this kid. He had Barbie dolls, too. She hated him, but she never did anything about it. Having a twin, we would talk about it. We were off to the gay bars together by 15 or 16.

Keith

I knew I was gay in fifth grade because I was sent out to the bench in the hall for being bad. I was in a combination fifth and sixth grade class, and one of the sixth graders was caught talking, too, and he was sent out on the lunch bench, too. He started looking at the hair on my arms, and he said, "I bet you have a lot of pubic hair." And I did in fifth grade 'cause I matured early and I remembered getting excited and thinking that I was different than everyone else. It's all trimmed off now.

Jackson

We got new draperies in the living room, this was the late 1970s. We lost the dramatic purple drapes to get beige or something. Well, I was in seventh grade and I told my mom I was sick and I turned those purple drapes into a dress All I did was remove the hooks and cut a circular hole, taped down the threads and belted it. And I ran around the house in this gown thing. I reenacted a chase scene and staged a rape scene as I was running down the hallway at home. I was all alone; God was watching my drama though.

Marcus

I was ten or 11, when I put on my sister's underwear and nylons and I wanted to dress as a woman for Halloween and my mom let me. She even made me up and put her wig on me. I went trick or treating. That was a clue. My parents knew I would throw a fit if they didn't let me. My mom just wanted me to be happy.

Daniel

They used to ask me when I was small about having a girlfriend and I always said, "I am never going to get married." They said, "Oh yes you will, you will fall in love." Well, I have fallen in love but not with a girl and I won't be getting married. This is my lover Kevin.

Mike

When I was painting my fingernails with her clear acrylic polish at seven years old. I did it in hiding in the bathroom and I hid my luxurious nails from them, with the clear polish.

At age four or five, when it was a macho thing for me, my dad and my brother and I went to pee in the toilet and I looked at their dicks. I remember that. My mom's a lesbian now.

Bill

I liked to get naked and put on my stepfather's underwear and I got the front wet with water and sucked the juice out of the front of it at 11 or 12. I remember thinking that was weird or different but it wasn't until years later that I realized it was an attraction to the same sex that had driven me.

Rick

This is a strange story. I went looking at pee puddles in the field. In Nevada where my family was living, I saw a car with three guys get out and take a piss. I was nine or ten and when they left I went to the site to see how big the puddles were... Big puddles meant big dicks. That was something weirdly sexual and homo.

Marc

38

I made my sister a dress, actually it was a skirt. I was five or six, and I made it all by hand. My mom took me to the store when I expressed a desire to do sewing. I picked out fabric and did it by hand. Our baby-sitter was a seamstress so I guess that's where I picked it up. It came out beautifully. Another time, my mom caught me in my sister's prom dress, the boa and all. I was six.

Neal

Okay, I'll just tell you what happened. I went over to my friend's house at about 13. And we'd go up into his room. And we'd be having sex in his bathroom, and his parent thought we were getting high on marijuana. So we'd go down and watch *Star Trek*, and then go back up in the bathroom and have some more sex, while they're still watching *Star Trek* on TV. They never found out, but we were in the bathroom long enough that they started thinking something suspicious was going on. Earlier, I had asked my mom if I could take a shower with my best friend and she said, "No." And I didn't understand why.

Herman

I can remember looking at the little drawings in the back of comic book magazines where they advertise sea monkeys and toys and I saw the drawings of ads that said gain muscles in three weeks and I got an erection. That was my first idea that I might be gay and I was only 11.

Fred

I can't remember what age it was, it was under ten, when I took an unusual interest in the anatomy of the Ken doll. Strangely, I wanted to be in the pool when there was a lot of men in the water and not with women. The key for me was being unusually, uncommonly attracted to male anatomy. That was the first moment when I realized that I was different.

Lane

I don't know if I did anything. I was closeted as a child. I read a lot as a kid, what else. I loved fairy tales, loved Disney classics. I can draw. I am a professional artist today. I used to draw these things constantly. I also loved musicals as a child and bought many movie soundtracks.

Then there is the time that I saw the movie *The Sound of Music* when I was about five years old and everyone in my family came out loving Maria, but I loved the Baroness. She had all the best dresses and all the best bitchy dialogue. They should have known then, I guess. They just couldn't understand why I didn't like the sweet little Maria. The Baroness was a bitch, I loved her. Scary, but telling.

Ian

Here in America you have to act really macho, everybody sees you as straight, but in Europe, men are more feminine. So my parents were surprised when I told them I was gay, because they thought I really liked girls. I was into sports and I did all those things which a straight guy's supposed to do.

I became a flight attendant, but for the airline I worked, 90 per cent of the male flight attendants were straight.

I was on the diving team in high school and it was required that I join the ballet. I was really scared because I knew in the ballet there were a lot of gay people, and I even told my parents that I was scared that I was going to turn gay because I was joining the ballet. And my mother told me that if I don't feel that way then I won't become gay, and if anybody tries to hit on me, just tell them no.

Later when I told them that I was gay, like years and years later, they said, "It's so funny because when you told us that you were scared to go in ballet, we never assumed you would ever be gay." I had a great childhood and I knew that my parents wouldn't be very upset when I told them, because they were very understanding parents, very open-minded.

My parents had an idea because suddenly only guys called and no girls. So my mother assumed something and I thought it was time to tell them. I was really scared, not that they would reject me but that they would kind of look differently at me or whatever. But they were just great. I think my mother had more of a problem with it than my father, because my father said, "You know, I thought it was something worse."

Johann, Austria

My parents made me play football when I was ten years old. I hated it, of course, but I did love my uniform. I didn't want to go to the football games 'cause I didn't want to get my uniform dirty. Clue number one. My parents clued in on that. I just loved the maroon jersey and the shoulder pads. I thought I looked very sharp, very butch. I went around with the shoulder pads on, throwing attitude like Joan Crawford.

Ralph

When I was about 12 years old, my mother found Polaroid pictures of me with a huge, swelling hard-on and she asked me to come in to talk. She said, "Mark, please come here I want to talk to you for a second." And I thought it was going to be a loving mother chat so I was like all happy. So I went in there and my mother asked me what these pictures were and I was like, "Well, can't you tell?" And she said, "Whose is this?" And I was like, "They're mine." And she said, "I don't ever want to see any of this behavior again, young man."

My father is gay. My little brother is gay. My sister is a lesbian, yeah, we're all gay. And my mother is a little bit insane. I grew up in Alabama. I twirled the baton from the age of like five, until I was about ten. I wanted to be a cheerleader in high school, but they wouldn't allow me, and I always wanted to do gymnastics, but boys weren't allowed to do that. And I don't know how I got to start ballet, 'cause boys weren't allowed to do ballet either. But now I'm a professional dancer in the world's most incredible ballet company in Frankfurt, Germany.

Mark

I used to pretend that all my pajamas were dirty so I could wear my mother's nightgown. I was eight or nine. That was a big giant sign.

My mother should have known I was gay when she came to visit me and stayed in my roommate's room and unknowingly on his shelf was a picture of me in a beaded gown and a tiara. I was 23. I purposely cleaned out the entire room of fag pictures, and incriminating evidence but left one, because it was convincing—I thought it looked like a girl. You could only see it when you were lying on the bed. Every night that she stayed, she sat and read and saw the picture. My mother never said a word. The world will never know if she recognized her son in that picture or not.

Larry

My earliest sexual memories are when an older boy in my neighborhood, he was probably about ten and I was about five, he took me to the basement of our building to the janitor's washroom. And we both stripped down to our underwear and kind of, did this kind of, well, like, it was kind of like Tarzan and Boy kind of thing. And then I remember we both got hard-ons, and he had me stroke his penis. He really got off on that. I couldn't, of course, couldn't have an orgasm yet, but he really like, loved that. If my mom had caught us, she would have known something was up.

Kevin

My best friend and I, we used to have fantasies about relationships. Like he would come into my bedroom and I would be lying on the bed naked, and he would come home from work and we'd say, "How was your day?" Talk about your day and he would lie on top of me. We used to do that all the time. We called it playing "N" for naked. That was our "N" game. Do you want to play "N" tonight? From six to 17 years old, we did it at least once a week. All made possible by the Catholic Youth Organization, I used to have sex with all my friends there, all my male friends.

Ron

I was never caught. My mother never walked in on anything. For some reason, she never thought I was gay, even when I told her, she thought it was a phase. I told her when I was 19. She had a major problem with AIDS, of course, fear. Her brother is gay, but I was having a relationship and she did not know how to handle it. She put me in counseling. I am 23 now. But at ten, I would have a certain friend over and spend the night and shut the door. Eventually things would happen and I hoped to God she would not open the door.

My stepsister put makeup on me when I was six and dressed me in heels. I do not think my Dad ever saw it, he would have gone through the roof. He does not like my gay uncle. My mother was so worried about AIDS 'cause my uncle is HIV positive. But the family accepts me today and they are very loving.

Joe

43

When I was 16, I went on a cruise to Bermuda with my parents and I was sitting on the sun deck and there was this guy in front of me. And he kept adjusting himself and lifting up his Speedos to give me a view. I was just about to leave when he started doing it. So, I hung out and we started talking. We had a little ship-board romance, a little ship-board sex. He had his own cabin so we would go down and use that. He had an extra cabin because he was with his fiancée. He was about 32. So that was fun.

Once when I lived with my parents, my mother was in my room and she found a card from this other guy I was dating. It had his picture in it and he signed it. His name was Shawn and she figured out he was a guy and he was gay. So she calls me up from work the next day and confronts me with it and says, "I found this card. And I was wondering..." And I said, "Yeah, Mom, I'm gay." Then she said something like, "How do you know? What about on the ship there were all these guys looking at you but you didn't talk to them?" I said, "Maybe I was looking back, Mom."

Kirk

When I was 15, I lived in my parents' place. And there was a delivery boy that worked for the butcher shop that used to come by all the time. He was really hot. I don't remember exactly how it happened, but I found out his name and looked up his phone number, and I used to phone him up and disguise my voice as a woman's voice. Eventually, it turned into phone sex. Finally the whole thing was getting a bit twisted, I decided I wanted to meet him. So I actually arranged a date. Slowly, over a long period of time, I was revealing more and more, and so was he; it was before commercial phone sex. We got to know each other and this guy wasn't stupid. He figured out that it was a boy. I wanted to meet and he did too. And we actually did meet one night and had sex in the back seat of his car. We had arranged to meet and he pretended that he didn't know that I was a boy. You know, he let me suck his dick or something. And that was it.

Niles

I think I was about 11. I had played football since I was five. I used to hang out and watch the other games. The high school was right across from my house. One day I had to pee, and I went to the urinal, and this athletic man was peeing next to me. Oh God. And my penis started getting hard, and so did his. So he went into a stall and I went in and he gave me a blow job. So I ran home and there was cum on the tip of my penis when I pulled out. That was the first time. I ran home, which was across the street, and I realized this is how you jerk off. I knew what I was doing and I wanted to do it. My grandmother showed me how to crochet and my mother showed me how to knit but I learned how to masturbate from a football player.

Clark

My mom always knew. Moms know. They just have this seventh sense. She went through my mail...13, I had a boyfriend. He was sending me love letters from West Covina, California, to far away Woodland Hills, California. We met in the food court of the mall in the year 1986. He was 19 and I was 13. He would come to all my football games and watch. I was almost 14, so it wasn't so bad. We went out for almost a year, then we broke up. He was writing me letters. I didn't know that because my mother was confiscating them. Yes, she was getting them all before I got them. She confronted me about my homosexuality, I told her I would change because she had a bad heart, and I didn't want her to have a heart attack. But I didn't change. I had sex in the bushes at the mall and these three girls walked in on us and started screaming. I used to get *Playgirl* from the store but she never knew about that. We kept them in our clubhouse. I was 11 when I did that. I had five brothers who found out but they never had a problem with it.

One of things people ask me since I played football is whether the team used to have like a group sex thing, but it never happened. I never looked at them. They were just my buddies. The first time I actually had intercourse I was in Hawaii. I was 14 and I didn't like it.

Hardy

Well, I'm a go-go dancer, so I got a love letter from a guy at my club, and my aunt found it and asked me 20 questions. Are you gay? Do you have a boy friend? Have you done it yet? Do you practice safe sex if you do? Simple questions. I did not answer her truthfully, no I didn't. It was hard to because I'm only 18 and I wasn't sure if I wanted to be with guys only or guys and girls. I had my first encounter with a guy when I turned 18. And I got blasted with all these questions from my aunt. I mean I hadn't even formulated all the questions in my own mind yet.

Ivan

When I was four years old, I used to take my mother's purse, a little one, and I would carry it around the house everywhere and walk on my tippy-toes. My father got real angry and screamed at me and grabbed the purse one time. But my mother said, "You give that back to him." She knew somehow. She was defending me. I'm black so you can imagine this big black strong mother saying, "You give that purse back to him."

Roger

I got into grandmother's jewelry box when I was five years old. And put on the pearls and the clip-on earrings and everything, and the rings, and I came downstairs and paraded in front of everyone. The family laughed. They thought I was funny. I was playing drag, wearing skirts and stuff when I was ten or 11. They never tried to stop me. Dad just kind of looked at me like I wasn't his.

Robert

I used to want to have sex with my father. He was bald and he would pay me quarters to massage his head. I used to fantasize about reaching down his back and touching his whole body. I was eight and loved to run around naked all the time in front of the neighbor kids. Streaking was big and I used to love to do that. I thought it was a great concept. I wouldn't let them see me, I would hide behind things.

Mom once dressed me as a little girl for Halloween. My sister is 14 months older than I am, and they always say, "Oh, you should have been a girl. You're so pretty." White pearls and a white dress for Halloween. There's a picture of me dressed like this. It's still humiliating when we look at the slides and that picture comes up.

Kip

My mother dated a football coach, since my father was dead, and he had been a professional football player. The coach would play football with me from the time I was eight. He wanted to lay my mom so he really was good to me. And he was huge. He came over in these coach's shorts and no shirt and he would say, "come boy and tackle me." I would wrap myself around him and rub my face in his crotch. For a long time this went on and I looked at the straps of his jock and I loved him.

And then at 13, my mom hired this other guy to look after me when the coach was gone. This new guy was a college wrestler and a football player. My mom was concerned that I didn't have a father figure. Once we were playing football and he knocked the wind out of me while we were playing football. So he straddled me and rubbed my chest and looked in my eyes. I got a boner and it hit me like a wave. I realized that I was gay. He went to Vietnam and got killed but he sent me a book back from Vietnam before he died. It was Paul Galliso—The Snow Goose and he inscribed it. He signed it...with love.

Ben

My mom said, "Randell, when you first told me that you were gay five months ago, I didn't want to believe you, but I do now." And I went, "That's a good thing, Mom. It's been a long time." And she said, "One time we were at Mary's house and all the girls were going to spend the night with all the sons, and you said, 'Mom, I can't sleep here, this house is too dirty.'" Now that is an indicator, okay.

Randell

I stole my mother's makeup and my sister's dress and there was this big scandal all around the family because they were blaming it on my other sister, but all the time it was me and I had hidden it. I was nine.

When she found gay porno magazines in my room at age 19, I told her, "That doesn't mean I'm gay, Mom." She believed me.

Ian

The last time someone came up to me and asked me a question like this, it ended up in the North Carolina Museum of Art. I was in a restaurant and this guy came up and dropped a pad and pencil on the table and said that a friend of his was doing an art project and wanted quotes on "what Raleigh meant to you." I was going through a tough time at this point because I was coming out to my parents and they weren't taking it very well. And so I wrote, "I came out in Raleigh" and signed my name to it. Well, a few months later a friend of mine went to the museum and saw that this artist had photographed this little thing that I had written and blown it up by two feet by three feet. And it was up on the wall in the main exhibit hall. It had my name on it and my mother was the head of her art guild from a small town in North Carolina and she organized a bus trip to see the exhibit, where my quote was on the wall. She found out about it and word got out quickly and she freaked, she totally freaked.

I went to a counselor to decide what to do, if I should say to my mother that she should just deal, "Mother, it's your problem, you have to deal with it," or if I should go to the artist and get him to remove the quote. But I didn't. So while this is all going on in North Carolina I went out to have a drink, this time I was in West Hollywood, and I was walking down the street, and there was Jay Leno, and he had these two little dolls. And one was dressed up like the gay Ken doll with the cock ring necklace. And he was asking gay guys on the street if they thought this was a gay doll or not. So I have become afraid of these interviews. In the end my mom's trip was mysteriously canceled. Go figure. And I never did call the artist.

Terry

When I was at an English boarding school, I had a major crush on my sports teacher for about four years. Then when I was 13, graduated to English public school, which is actually a private school, I had a crush on a different sports teacher. The public school is notoriously strict. They produce three kinds of people:
1. heterosexual sex maniacs,
2. asexual boring straight people, and
3. very funny and communicative homosexuals.

You have to guess which one of the three I am, bearing in mind I'm sitting here at this very moment at a gay beach in California, thousands of miles from where I live now, 'cause I'm on vacation. I'm working out here. You tolerate homosexuality a little differently here in the United States than in England. It's a little like the armed forces here "Don't ask, don't tell." In England, that's how it is with homosexuality.

Jack

When I went to church with my grandmother, she used to wear these long, white gloves and I would put them on. I was very short then, but I would reach my hands up into the air and conduct the choir. Folks in the church said they didn't see me, just my dancing hands sticking up from out of the pews. This was like pre-puberty, like nine years old.

Greg

When I was 16 years old, I used to fool around with the quarterback from the football team at his house. Finally, he asked me to have full-on sex. "Put it in," that's what he said. "Put it in." After I put it in him with like Vaseline, his mother came in downstairs. And she kept yelling, "Terry, Terry." And he kept saying, "Keep going, she won't come up here for a while. She has to put away the groceries." I was terrified. Having sex with him for the first time and his mother downstairs. I came soon after that, so there wasn't much to keep going for.

Wayne

When I was about eleven, I used to dance in my bedroom alone to Donna Summers, while my brothers were in the next room listening to Led Zeppelin. Back then I was just dancing around, listening to Gloria Gaynor sing "I Will Survive." And I knew I would. And I have, baby. Today I live in Newport Beach, California, and I'm a beautiful blond with Ray-Bans and a "Get Out America" T-shirt on.

Bob

My mother knew when I was four years old that I must be a homosexual because my favorite album was *Madame Butterfly* excerpts. I used to force my grandmother, my aunts, anybody that could read to read me the back cover: the entire plotline, including the ending. I forced everybody in the house to listen to the great Puccini opera. I used to like the part where Madame Butterfly would kill herself at the end. The soprano would be like screeching these notes out. It's really very beautiful .

Around 19 years old, one of my brothers who's terribly homophobic made a nasty comment about homosexuals; I, of course, made my announcement to the entire family that they were talking about me, if they were putting people into that classification...and, of course, it sent shivers down everybody's spine.

Clint

I was washing and cleaning a cucumber to make salad and for some reason I had to go up to my room and get something. Unwittingly, I wrapped the cucumber in a towel and ran upstairs to my room. I was in my closet digging around and apparently I put down the cucumber there in the closet. Because a few hours later my Mom was getting the dirty laundry out of my closet and she found it. My mom and sister came and found the cucumber. My mom and my sister were laughing, and yelling, "Pat, come up, come up." They were laughing and saying like, "What's this?" Truthfully, I was just washing it. Not that I hadn't...maybe tried it before.

Oscar

So I had just turned 16 and it was the summertime in Visalia, California. My job was to mow the lawns twice a week. Well, I have allergies, so I have to pretty much deck myself out in the gear that would prevent me from swelling up in terrible places, right. I wore a gas mask that would go over my face. I would have glasses on. During the lawn mowing, it was a huge lawn, I would get bored and I would put earphones on. So I had earphones, glasses, and a gas mask and nothing else but little tiny shorts and thongs. Shorts, no underwear. Tiny, tiny, little shorts. So as I was mowing the lawn with the glasses, the mask and the whole thing. This guy on the bike rode by with the small shorts and no shirt, and he had to be like 26. He was gorgeous, tan and a little hairy chest; I was just dying. He was kind of meandering by, there's a dead end on my street so I knew he had to come back.

I ripped all my stuff off, the sunglasses, the radio and the gas mask, and I took the thongs off. And I kind of brushed myself off and combed and tried to make myself look respectable or sleazy, whichever he would prefer. As he rode by again, I stopped and I leaned up against the lawn mower, and I just kind of watched him. And as he got further down the street I whistled at him. Really loud whistle. And he kept going real slow, I watched and he was gone. And I thought damn, he's gone. Then as I started the lawn mower back up, I saw his bike snaking his way back down the street again, I thought, "Hmm, this is interesting." So I stopped the lawn mower again, and I was pretending I was doing something else, you know, very important, but very close to the street so I could get a good look when he came by.

So he came up and he said, "Hi, do you know where such-and-such street is?" Well, I had been in that city all my life and I knew that city like the back of my hand, and there was no street that he had mentioned, right. So at this point I knew that something was up. And I said, "Well, I don't think there's a street called that, but where are you going? What general area?" Well, he said he lived in Solaria and he biked down to Visalia which is where I lived. It's about ten miles and you can bike that, so it's no big deal. So he had biked to Visalia and he was riding around. Well, I said, "Why don't you come inside so you can call?" 'Cause he was going to his girlfriend's house, of course, it was his girlfriend. And I said, "You can come inside and use the phone if you want."

And he came inside, I had the ulterior motive to get him in the house and cook him later. So as he went inside, my parents were gone, of course, I jumped in the pool, I took off my shorts and jumped in the pool to get all the dirt and stuff off me from mowing the lawn. When I went back inside and I was toweled off, I had a towel on, and we started talking. We sat at the table. Nothing was said. We talked about his girlfriend, college, sports and girlfriends, and then, out of the blue, he tells me, "Well, can I get a tour of your house?"

And I was like, well, he caught me off guard, but sure why not, what the hell. So I take him around, this is the living room, the television and he looked like he had absolutely no interest. He bee-lined to my bedroom. Sat down on the floor, and goes, "Oh, my back hurts so bad. I would love a massage." Well, at this point it was pretty obvious what was going on, but we were playing at it so slow and so innocuously that at this point we both could have been straight. So I start giving him a back rub and he was talking about his tennis career and how he gets real bad back pains from the tennis instructor and his girl friend and this and that. And as I'm rubbing his back, I'm getting this huge hard-on. And at some point during the back rub it was pretty clear that both of us were excited and he turned around and we proceeded to obviously enjoy the experience of each other. In the most intimate way, you know. And needless to say we got to the point where I made him howl, which was great for me.

After we were through and squee-geeing off the appropriate parts of our body that needed squee-geeing off, my mom came home. This man who had been lying there absolutely senseless, in a stupor for five minutes, sprung up out of bed, grabbed his clothes, threw his pants on and climbed out my window. So I have foot marks on the wall and he gets out the window and he tears off through the azaleas and his bike's in front. So he has to sneak around to the front of the

53

house where my mom is coming in, grab his bike and tear off down the street. Unbeknownst to my mom, I'm tucking my shirt in and cleaning up the mess that had just been made and playing it cool. That was it. She didn't know, she didn't have a clue. He was hot. He was about 6' 2", and he was like about 26 years old, short dark hair. He was a tennis pro, and he had a great body. He said he had a girl-friend, but anyone that enjoyed taking my parts like that obviously knew what he enjoyed.

Brent

I used to play in the basement of my parents' house. I would wear this cloth over my head and pretend it was hair and I was a female. I used to talk to myself and play these stories when I was a girl. One time my mother opened the cellar door and said, "What are you doing down there?" Really angrily. And I said, "Nothing, nothing." And she repeated the question a couple times. And I was really ashamed and I felt caught. And I used to listen to a lot of Broadway musicals when I was seven or eight, "Hello Dolly" and other show tunes like that. I listened to classical music, too, and they thought that was kind of strange.

Austin

My mother was assistant scoutmaster for a boy scout troop that I was in. She should have known when I was the boy leader of the scout troop. We had a separate patrol for the older scouts and we stayed in a two-man tent. I made it this big thing that everyone of the eight guys had to stay in this two-man tent. So what we did, since it was too hot, we laid the sleeping bags out and we all messed around.

There was one time when my mother needed me for something in the middle of the night and she came to the tent and she saw what was going on. She asked what we were doing and I said the classic "noth-ing." That was it, she went back to her tent and didn't talk to me the rest of the night.

Pete

At nine, there is a photograph of me in my mother's nightgown with balloons as breasts and a big balloon as a butt. The whole family was there and it was before Christmas.

I have always known, but I was always careful not to let others know. Once, my brother screamed at me when I called his GI Joe "a doll." He said, "GI Joe is a soldier not doll." I cried a lot from the loneliness and the people who were making fun of me at school. I made my *Six Million Dollar Man* doll have sex with Ken and sometimes with Barbie. I played Barbie with my sister and I think I had more fun than she did. Also, I used to roller skate and play hula hoops which only the girls did. I used to go downstairs hide in the bathroom and play with Barbie. All I wanted to do is dress Barbie in a gown.

Going to the baseball games was a fiasco. For me it was all about trying to act interested in the game when really I was just interested in looking at the players and the fans.

Wilson

My brothers and sisters were with me on Halloween. We went to the door and said, "Trick or treat." The woman said, "What are you?" My brother said, "I'm a ghost." My sister said, "I'm a witch." And I said, "I'm Beverly." That's when they should have known I was gay. I was dressed as my father's boss' secretary. I thought she was so pretty. I was seven years old. This happened in rural Massachusetts. Later, one of my boyfriends called me at the house when I was 19. After he talked to my mother, she said, "Oh, he has a nice voice." Little did she know...

Jose

Once, I walked into the house and the hall was all shut and closed off and I walked into the hall and walked around the corner and my brother was preening in my sister's first prom dress in front of a full length mirror. And I just started laughing and he turned around and screamed and ran into his room in a cloud of chiffon. Orange chiffon, it was beautiful. I'm still not sure if I'm gay, I'm 35 and I'm living with my mother at home, and my brother's gay now. Probably from the orange chiffon.

Jerry

My mother used to make me sing to Shirley Bassey records when I was six, "Diamonds are Forever." She would make me put her dressing gown on back to front. She did as well, she put the same thing on and we'd sing together. And we'd sing into the end of the vacuum cleaner. And we'd do all of the actions with our hands, too. This happened in my mother's house in the living room lounge in London, England, in 1975. My mom is very camp; an air hostess, she was. She retired only a few years ago. We used to have a Jack Russell terrier dog and I used to dress it up with my mother's wigs and clip on earrings on his ears. And he would shake them off. We put him in the wheel barrow and would wheel it around the garden and pretend it was a princess, me and my twin brother, he's straight. When I told her I was gay, she loved it. She was happy, because she worked with a lot of gays and she knew what it was all about. I was 15 years old when I told her. I figured it out, because when I was in the showers at the cricket games or at the soccer games, my willy would get a little bit bigger and I realized that something was different about me. Now I live in London and I'm a flight attendant for Virgin Airlines.

Kelvin

I probably listened more intently, was more interested in what was happening in her life and with her friends when she gossiped and things. When I was 15 and he was 14, I used to sleep with my cousin naked and my other brother didn't do that. She might have known then. She actually did say something, she tried to stop us. She said, "How come you're sleeping naked?" I don't know how she knew, she must have walked in the room one night. And I was embarrassed. I walked away and went in my room and shut the door and I didn't talk to her.

Justin

I tried on my sister's wedding gown when I was 12 and ripped the side. I never got in trouble. They were wondering how it got ripped, but they never found out how. To this day they don't know. They don't know that I'm gay either.

Zale

I guess they should have wondered when I took the pants off the gardener. We had a gardener. We had a rather big place and I was highly curious, excited maybe, and I was four years old. He was reading the comics on Sunday morning and he didn't have a shirt on. I would always play piggy back on him, so I decided this time I would unlatch his pants and slide off the back and pull his pants down. He was 26. He was pissed and he told me he was going to tell my mom. That's when I threatened him with deportation and he never told my mom. My parents still haven't found out I'm gay.

Carl

57

I tried to penetrate a knot hole once in a tree and I got sore because I couldn't get it out. I got splinters in me. I was like 14 or 15. Eventually because of the splinters I lost my erection, but I was stuck there for many minutes. It seemed like more than it was, probably. By age 21, I was already in a relationship for four years with a guy. I was 17 and he was 52, and it lasted 17 years.

Paul

I waited until my mom was gone and I used to run around naked. I was 11 years old. I thought it was exciting to run around naked. I actually jumped up and down on my mom's bed, springing on her bed. I think I was so repressed as a child that doing something like that was erotic. This happened in New York City.

Alister

I have an older brother who's gay and he said he knew I was gay as soon as I started listening to Barbra Streisand when I was 14 or 15 years old. He was nine years older than me. Also I used to play with dolls as a kid, little troll dolls. My mother said she knew I was gay because I didn't date girls in high school.

Winston

My father was like the big macho, football-player type, and we didn't have a dishwasher as a kid. So my mother trained us, and I was the oldest. When my sister hit five, she became the dryer and I was the dishwasher. My father thought it was funny that my mother was relaxing and I was doing the dishes and my sister was drying. And I was always running around straightening up and keeping our house in order. Everyone in our house was throwing things everywhere and it drove me crazy. My father would look in the kitchen and see me doing the dishes and say, "Marlon, you're going to make someone a great wife someday." Today, I'm a 195-pound muscular man and I'd still make a great wife.

Marlon

I remember fighting with my mother at Halloween time because I wanted to be a witch instead of a warlock. She made a fuss over that when I was six years old in Fairfax, Virginia.

They should have known I was gay when, at ten, I couldn't stop rearranging the living room furniture. I remember I used to baby-sit a bunch of kids and dress them up in my sister's gowns and make them do these dances that I choreographed and beauty pageants. I put makeup on them. Recently, my little sister was talking to my best friend Sue, and she said, "I knew he was gay since he was about three feet tall because he used to like to dress up in Mom's clothes."

Earl

I opted for drama instead of sports when I was in school, in England. I started fooling around with guys when I left home and went to college when I was 18. I guess she should have known when I brought home my first roommate, and he was like a Greek god. We were fooling around, we were lovers. He's an actor who works occasionally. You see him on TV in bits and pieces. His name is Andy. She said, "Oh my God, that Andy, he's wonderful, but I guess he's gay, right?" She didn't know that I had had an affair with him for a year when we were in college together.

Gary

We had some neighbors across the street that used to baby-sit us when we were very, very young because my parents were working. The couple was in their 40's. That was in the late '60s. And for some reason they used to carry this huge black purse. I was five and I used to steal the purse. They wouldn't let me have it and I would steal it and play with it in my room. The funny part about it is it wasn't even fashionable.

I knew I was gay when I was ten. I could tell that I had a very strong attraction to men. By the time I was 12 years old, I was sexually active.

Darick

59

I was a very inquisitive child at age 13 and I wanted to find out things about being gay but I didn't know where to go and how to find things out. So I would just go up to people and ask them if they were gay. One summer I went away to camp and there was a counselor who I thought could possibly be gay. He was maybe 23 years old. I went up to him one day and said, "Are you gay by any chance?" That was my line back then. And he said, "yeah," but he was all nervous like he thought that everyone else knew or thought he was gay or that they were talking about him. But I told him that no I was just curious and

I had a feeling. He calmed down and then took me back to the gymnasium. It was really dark and we went downstairs. I guess he had done this before because there was a bottle of Vaseline in this little hidden area. We were in a gym, below the basketball court with hard wood floors. Anyway, then he realized that it wasn't cool there so we went back to his place. Before I left, he penetrated me. It hurt a lot and I could barely walk home. I was nervous that the other people from the camp might notice that I was walking funny or something or that I had done something.

That same summer, there was someone who I roomed with who was very effeminate and I knew he was gay. He was older, maybe 18. Every time I would try to bring up the subject he would say, "never, never ask me that" and so I got rebellious inside because I needed to talk about it. So one day I went through his drawers and I found some *Playgirl* centerfolds, about 20 of them. Being that I was mad, I took them and I showed his centerfolds to all my friends. Looking back in retrospect it wasn't a very nice thing to do, but I wanted someone to talk to.

Then I lived in Long Island and there wasn't any gay hotlines back then and I found out quite by accident that there was this gay bar named Stars and it was 20 minutes from where I lived. When I got my license I would drive by it. I used to work at night nearby so I would go back via Stars and just sit and watch and hear the music and stuff. One day, wanting to know more about being gay, I called up and talked to a bouncer type gay guy and he agreed to meet me. We met at my high school on a Saturday and he ended up taking me into his white Trans Am. He was a light skinned black guy, something that didn't turn me on, and I got very nervous and he tried to take me to bed but I wasn't into it so he respected that. He talked to me and answered questions that I had. Questions like how guys had sex and actually how guys knew that another guy was gay. He said, "I could be in a room with ten guys for an hour and I could come out of there and know exactly which guys were gay and which were not." I said, "how could you know?" I couldn't believe that. I said, "do they wear their hair a certain way or wear clogs or was it the earring thing because the real gay guys like the Village People or whatever if they were blatant they would wear clogs or earrings or had real close-cut hair." Those were the signals I thought, but he said, "no, no, you will know" and now I realize that what he said is true but back then it fascinated me.

I used to go to the beach with my sister. We would go to Robert Moses beach and I would take these long walks. I guess I knew that there was a nude beach. When I saw guys by themselves I would go up and ask them my famous question, "Are you gay by any chance?" Everyone was really nice! I mean there was one guy who said, "No, I am sorry I am not gay; I am sorry because you are really cute...I wish I was." There was no one who said, "get out of here I'll kill ya," I was 16 at the time, very precocious.

Then I remember being in line at the snack bar at the beach and there was a guy in line and I remember that he had a football under his arm and he looked at me. He looked at me piercingly and walked out and then I went, oh my God he was looking at me because he was cruising me. I ran out to try to find him and eventually I did find him and he looked at me and I look at him and then he started going up into the dunes and I followed him and we had sex in the dunes. He was from Canada and his comment afterwards was that I was going to be an asset to gay society. I had sand everywhere; having sex in the sand is not a fun thing.

I used to go into New York City; I got a little more brave and I told my mom I was going to the city on the train with my friend Jean to the New York Public Library. I would make up these imaginary friends like Jean. I would end up going to the Adonis theater or the Eros theater because I realized they had gay movies there and I thought, wow this is really cool. At first, I didn't go right in because I didn't think I was old enough and I was scared but one day a guy came out and he looked like the hottest and huskiest looking guy. I said this guy can't be gay. No, no, I can't believe it, he looks like a football player. So I followed him and I followed him and he went into a hotel; it was the Hotel Wellington. I went into the lobby and I lost him and I was just about to leave when someone tapped me on the shoulder. It was him. He said, "do you want to come up to my room?" and I said "Oh my God, I can't believe it." He was from Johannesburg, with a hot stocky football player build, and he told me that his father owned Air Italia Airlines; I don't know if that is true, but anyway. He, like the other guys that I met, wanted to penetrate me. I was 17 then and he did and I remember spending a lot of time in New York picking up people as they left the theater. That was my way. I told my mom I was at the library. I was a junior in high school; it was 1979 and I didn't enjoy having sex that way. I think that is what turned me off to it. Having that kind of sex early and hating it saved me from getting AIDS.

Ted

Hi! I'm Mike and I am 19 years old and just came out about three years ago. My family didn't do anything about it, but also don't like it. It's crazy that my family didn't know I was gay. I'm going to tell a few stories now. I am glad that there is a book like this for us to tell our stories.

It began when I was about 11, when I was collecting undergear that were other men's, and my mother found them. I was wearing them and smelling them. I told her I found them. She said okay and I thought I was caught.

My mother should have known I was gay when at age 12 I seduced my older brother and gave him head every night that he was living with us.

When I was about 17, when my mother and father started finding pictures of guys in my room and phone calls to gay 900 numbers.

When at age 18, I was wearing three earrings and having sex with guys in the living room and watching gay videos, when my parents were out. When she caught me in the act a few months later then she really should have known.

Mike

I have a story. My family is very religious and we used to go to Sunday school when I was a kid. And we had the cloth felt things where they put up the Biblical characters. One time when I was home I put my blanket over my head and I was pretending to be Mary and my parents would see me walking around the house with my blanket over my head. And they would ask me what I was doing and I would say I was pretending to be Moses. But really I was pretending to be Mary. My mom even has pictures of me, but I never told her the truth. I was four years old and I knew I was lying, but even today I never told them I was actually Mary and not Moses. I will never tell her because it's something she loves to talk about. She thought it was so cute. Also when I was little I liked to clean and she said, "Someday you'll make some girl a really good wife."

Dale

I suppose that I was about ten or 11. Our neighbor was about 15 or 16 and on the high school football team. His parents worked and so did my mother (my parents were divorced). Each afternoon after school we would start by him suggesting we should wrestle. One thing would lead to another and eventually we would both be naked and I would go down on him, which he loved. This went on for a couple of years after school. Richard even started to either jack me off or go down on me, I can only remember once that he penetrated me; he used soap as a lube. I loved it. I was sent to live with my grandmother when I was 13 and my mother died. At 16, I went to live with my father and his boyfriend; my father was gay also.

Being raised in a gay household in Australia was interesting to say the least. Lots of parties and lots of sex. I didn't know if my father ever knew that I was sleeping with his friends but in the back of my mind I think he did. Anyway, having sex with my father's friends went on for years until I left for university where a few of the female teachers took a liking to me. One in particular. We were married on my 19th birthday. It lasted four years.

I then came out in a major way. My father was thrilled to say the least. I have three half brothers from my dad's second marriage, and two of these guys are gay. My dad died about two years ago, his boyfriend and I keep in close contact and I love him like he was my second father. I also did and still do very good lip-synch to all of the Barbra Striesand and Shirley Bassey records that my dad and his lover Paul had. By the way Richard's marriage lasted 4 years and I see him all the time here in Sydney, Australia. When I was about 16, I started finding dad and Paul's porno magazines; of course, as any 16 year old would do, I jacked off to them, never realizing that my cum would stain things if not cleaned up properly. We had white carpet. I'll leave the rest up to your imagination but questions were asked by my father.

Jerome

I borrowed my Mom's VCR and when I gave it back to her a few weeks later, I forgot and left a gay porno movie in the VCR. She told me the next day that she watched the entire two hour video and she thought that it was very interesting. She is completely supportive of my gay rights. Though she is not sure how to be or when to be open about it. She is a member of PFLAG.

Douglas

My object of desire was my best friend in high school and I realized one night when I was driving home that I was in love with him, and I thought I'd better tell him. So when I told him, he said "so am I" and we started sleeping together right away. My mother had a lot of difficulty with it which surprised me because I thought she would be fine. She was just worried about me. She thought it would restrict my career possibilities. My father asked me if I was gay. I barely remember what I said. I was 17. I think my father said, "Are you two boyfriends?" and I was pretty surprised and said "yes." He said, "What's wrong with you guys anyway?" And that was the end of it. He was fine. This was in Wisconsin, a small town.

Greg

I used to do funny things that should have been good indicators to my parents, like walk around in the front yard in my mom's high heels. She would get mad at me because I would get mud on the spike heels.

One winter my lover and I and were having trouble with our furnace and it got cold and we were waiting for the repairman. I had been living with my lover for three or four years. We hadn't come out to my parents even though they knew we owned a home together they just chose not to address it. My partner talked to my mom and was explaining to her how the furnace wasn't working. My mom, being the practical person she was, her advice was that we should sleep together to stay warm. His response was "Yeah that's a really good idea." Of course, we were sleeping together for a long time before that, but coming from my mom it was really very funny.

Pete

Ten or 11 years ago was my last holiday with my parent. I would go to Spain to the beach and see a lot of nice men and my mom would say there are nice girls here why are you watching the men. She wondered why I watched the men instead of the women. That was my mistake. I was 15. The next year we didn't talk about it when I went to the beach. I think my mother knew but I never told them. My parents are from the South of Germany and I live in the North, but we vacation in Spain.

Hans

In high school I was always dating girls, but at the same time I was chasing boys around too, in a small town in Indiana. I didn't really know that I was gay, but I knew that I was attracted to men at a very young age. My earliest childhood memories and homosexual experiences were with other boys, at five years old when we played with each other's willys, and that continued all through high school. I was dating this one particular girl and on one evening we had gone out and had sex, and after I left her house I went out to my little buddy's house out on the farm and knocked on his window and got him to

come out. Then we went out to the field and did it. We did just about everything. I don't know where I picked it up. I had seen straight porno. He had a great body, this hot little farm boy, excellent body, big schlong and I would say dirty words, have sex and spank him as I was doing it. It was very hot.

Billy

In 1949, I attended the fourth grade at a rural schoolhouse in Concord, Michigan. One day, I took my sister's lovely blue-covered, gold-lined cheer-leading dress, which fit down over my knees, to the 1860 built schoolhouse and changed in the cloakroom. I wore my usual underwear underneath, that seemed unimportant. But I loved the freedom of my legs and the way the skirt did so many things when

I walked. I do not remember one criticism or any reference to it by anybody except two good friends, guys, who asked me how I felt. I told them and showed them. I always wondered if they went home and tried it. But the amazing thing is that it was no a big deal. Mrs. Hoxie, the teacher, barely noticed.

I always loved that skirt. My sister was glad I did. She now works for the EEOC and the NAACP. The area near Concord, Michigan is horrid with prejudice now. I grew up there and from 16-19 knew drag queens and hustlers, hustling myself. Leather people have always been my favorite because I found them more intelligent people to hang around. They knew opera, movies, literature, and had great advice. My testosterone level was far too high to go into drag (uglier than Magnani!), too much body hair; I never did want to do drag again, but I remember that dress. Always!

I always wanted to be an opera singer (the costumes! And lack of them!) But no matter how I tried, singing was impossible. Ah, that cheer-leading dress. I am a lace maker today, crochet (museum quality), knitting and various bobbin laces; I am in museum collections and displays throughout the country. Still I prefer not to wear a dress around the house, apartment or studio, but wear a long shirt instead...naked underneath.

Victor

I was doing a boy named Bobby, penetrating him when I was in second grade and my mom walked in on us. I'll never forget this. She denies it. She said, "I hate your guts." Something like that. I'll never forget it.

You know I always did up the dolls hair. Everybody thought I was going to be a hair stylist, because seriously I would do the curlers. Then I would do my sister's hair and my mother's hair. When I was 13, I stopped that crap. That was when I wanted to be a cop. Then I was a piglet, a junior cop, in my town from 13 to 17. Then I was in the military and a military policeman for seven years.

From the age of ten to 17, there was about ten of us having sex practically every day in the town of Duarte, California. We'd hang out with an old troll, an old gay guy named Ken. He'd let us all go into the backroom and orgy out. And he got his kicks because he got to suck the little boys peepees. He let me ditch school and hang out at his house when he was working and the other boys would ditch school and we'd do our sex thing. Ken was in his 40's; he educated me. He never did anything with me. I used to steal all of his boyfriends and he kicked me out and wouldn't let me come over for a year. Then I was back in the "orgy room," that's what we called it.

Recently I ran into one of these guys at a doughnut shop and talked to him about the past, when I was 12 and he was nine and I started him off. When he hit puberty he got so big. I remember he would not let me suck him, he would only suck me and it was his idea. It was night time and I was on the side of Ken's house. I could see why he was at a doughnut shop; he was a real porker, fat.

Stuart

In school we had a book that showed people at different ages: the child, the adolescent and the man. I noticed I was interested in the men's pictures and not the women's.

Bernd, Germany

I don't want anyone to know that I danced in my underwear to Barry Manilow, singing along to "Copacabana" but that was one cool song. I used to go to a gay roller skating rink in the Valley when I was a teen. They gave out these pink slips and you could get a discount. I didn't want them because I was afraid I would lose them and my parents would find out. Wouldn't you know one of those pink things was found, and my mom came into my room. She always had to have these deep philosophical discussions at 2 am. She said, "Where did you get this?" She asked me if I was gay. I thought, "Sure I'm gay. Can I go back to sleep now?" She said, "I want you to know I'm okay with this." And that was it.

Gerald

When I was little there was a wedding at our house, and I was about five and I had this tendency to hit men in the balls. So I was banned that day from playing with the men, so I had to play with the girls. They were building these altars and were putting pictures of who they were going to marry on them and my mom went around and was checking them out and asking everyone who they were going to marry. She finally came around to me and I said I was going to marry Elvis Presley. Well, we didn't play wedding anymore. I recently reminded my mom about that and she denies remembering it.

Bill

I was kind of late the first time I was with a guy. I was 19. It was someone I worked with and it was a bunch of people in the mountains at my parents' cabin. It was both of our first times. Everybody got pretty drunk and we went on a hike in the woods. He was 17. I guess I could go to jail for it. My mother kept bugging me about it and she kept jokingly asking me and one morning she called me 6:30 am and she pissed me off so I just told her I was gay and that shut her up. Then there were two years of problems with my parents.

Otto

I used to go in my mother's closet and try on all her clothes and high-heeled shoes. In third grade, I had a big crush on my science teacher Mr. Skinner. He was beautiful.

When I was 15, there was this guy on the football team who came into the store where I worked in sweats and I used to stare at his dick and I couldn't figure out why. I should have known. Greg, my best friend in high school went to college 45 minutes away from me. I went to visit him once and he introduced me to a friend of his, who he informed me was gay. But this guy was very nice even though he was gay. I was straight at the time. I said, "okay; I don't care." The gay guy said, "I come to the city where you go to school to visit a friend of mine. Maybe I can visit you next time too." I said sure. A few weeks later he called and said he was coming to visit and then he asked me if he could stay with me, which was fine since my room-mate was going home that weekend. We went out and had drinks and came back. We were lying there and he asked if I had ever thought about having sex with a man. I said not really (what a liar!) and he asked if I wanted to have sex with him. I started shaking uncontrollable from excitement literally. I was in convulsions so he got off the bed and sat next to me. I was so excited and scared and he came over and undressed me. He asked if I was afraid and I said that I was excited. After we had sex, he said, "I thought you said you'd never done this before?" I said, "I never have had sex with a man before and only once with a woman." He said, "You did it just like a pro." At the time, I figured that was a compliment.

Thomas

I was in the bath with my cousin at age five and I stood up and instead of going to the lavatory for a pee, I peed on his head. It took him a while to realize because he is vague, and he didn't get up or move he just put his hand up over his head. I also shoved a perfume bottle up my backside. And my aunt walked in and I said, "I stuck a bottle up my backside." And she just looked at me and shook her head. It hurt. Then she called my mom and said, "Jane, Bert's got a bottle up his back side." Another story I've got is when I came home from boarding school at age 16 and my brother was using a vibrator to get the blood circulating around his head because he was going bald. I, in my devious manner, used it for something else; it was a very square object that I used to wank with. You could also use the attachment to stick it on the outside of your bum. One time, I forgot to wash it and my brother used it and he thought something had gone wrong with his hair. Because he felt his head and it was sticky and gross.

One time my father happened to catch me having a wank. There I was flat on my bed on a Saturday night going hammers and poggles hell bent for leather and my father opened the door and looked in, he hasn't entered my bedroom without knocking since.

Bert, Australia

71

I was old, probably 12. I'm embarrassed to say this. Remember the hair dryers with all the tubes and the big separate motor? Well I wanted to dry my hair this way. I was sitting there with the hair drier plastic bag on my head and my brother walked in, took one look, said, "Jesus," slammed the door and walked out.

Dennis

I always knew I was gay. The first time I really thought about it was when I actually looked up the word homosexual in the dictionary at age eight. I knew it was me.

Ralph, Germany

72

I'm 24, I was born in Turkey but have lived in Australia since I was two. I think I knew I was gay since about four or five, but didn't really understand it. When I was in kindergarten, there was a little girl and you could see under her dress and that turned me off. I used to knit, crochet, play with all the girls in school, hopscotch, paddy cakes I was better than the girls. It's hard when you're young and think you're the only one in the world. When I was about eight, my three brothers and I would play and get real dirty, awful really, and my mother would get upset and put us in the bathtub and scrub every inch of us. One day I decided not to get dirty anymore. I would wander around and gather flowers for mom. She was stunned.

I ran away from home and she kept trying to convince me that no one would marry a runaway. I told her I was never, ever, ever getting married, not now, not when I'm 30, 40, 50 never. Do you understand what I am trying to tell you? And there was silence on the other end of the phone for about a minute. So she asked my sister if I slept with boys, which Sister denied even though she knows I do.

Arjan

When I was four or five, I had a crush on this actress who is a bit of a gay icon now. At the end of her show she would come to the edge of the stage and raise her arms. My mother had coffee mornings and she would get me to copy that and show it to all her friends and they quite liked it.

Rob, London

My mother had me when she was 16 years old. I was playing with Barbies at six. I was playing with my girl cousins more than my boy cousins. Mom was a cocktail waitress. She had these outrageous outfits and I loved them and I used to walk in her heels. She was a go-go mom—French maid outfits and leather boots that came up past the knees. It was the 1970s and I thought it was really cool that my mom was so off-beat.

Craig

I went on a camping trip with my dad to the Kern River for white-water rafting. We spent the night on the river. I met this 16 year old boy; I was 13. We became really good friends and we set up our tents right next to each other. I went to sleep and pretty soon someone was crawling in my tent. I was afraid, so I pretended to be asleep. He did what he wanted, touching me. The next morning I couldn't look at him. I realized I enjoyed it. I decided to pursue the life of being with men. My parents blamed themselves at first, but after therapy they understood and accepted. My brother and sister were more athletic than me, so my parents were a little suspicious. I didn't play with Barbie or anything.

Kip

I grew up in Southeast Asia, in the war-torn country of Cambodia. I have been in America since 1981. I was a virgin until I was 22. I always knew. When I came out to my mother, she said she knew so I didn't have to explain anything. In my culture parents arrange marriages but I would never agree. When my mother was pregnant with me she thought I was a girl. As a toddler she even dressed me up as a girl and let me play with the other girl babies and I was often mistaken for a girl. My senior year in college I finally started dating. I saw a lot of guys in the shower but I never did anything about it. I was a gymnast and a competitive volleyball player, tennis, dance and swimming.

Gille

Once when I was on vacation at 14 years old, I had sex with a tour guide at Ruby Falls, Tennessee, 200 feet underground in a cave. It was near Chattanooga. He was very tall. We went down the elevator into the cave. Every once in a while during the tour, the two tour groups would pass each other and the rule was the group going into the cave would wait for the others to leave. I was first in line and the tour guide had a flashlight and when the first group went by the tour guide started rubbing it against my crotch. I was 14 and he was 18.

74

We continued and when the next group came by, he did it again. I felt this sensation again. I was too embarrassed to look down because my parents were right behind me. So I just stood there. When the next group went by, he had his hands there and he was grabbing me. At one point the recorded message talks about how the cave originally looked and the lights went out, and he was grabbing and fondling me and it felt good so I reached over and grabbed him and he said don't do that now because the lights are going to come on. And right then the lights came on. He told me to meet him in the bathroom later and I did. He asked me out. And I said, "Out? Boys don't go out together." In the bathroom, He sucked my dick and I went down on him for maybe three seconds, that was it. He turned me on so much. He had the biggest dick. I remember comparing it to the size of my wrist. It was huge. I was a nervous wreck. Finally, my family got in the car and went to get something to eat, but I stayed in the car 'cause I told my mother that I was sick. I stayed in the car and jacked off. My mother was there and she knew something was up. Much later she mentioned to her friends that the tour guide and I became very close. They've known since I was a kid. I was a nelly queen. I didn't play football or any sports and that is a dead give away. I liked to paint and garden, so they bought me weights to make me straight. It didn't work

Brad

I was on the family couch with the rest of the family watching TV and I was masturbating under a blanket to a beautiful man that was on TV. I was 15 year old, it didn't take long for me to come. I think I was always kind of different. I had girls as friends. I used to do weird things like play Helen Reedy "I am woman, hear me roar." Most 12-year-old boys don't do that. When I was ten, I locked myself into my room and listened to Olivia Newton John and pretended that I was her. In college, I double dated with my best friend from the Lambda Chi fraternity, then we would drop off the girls and have sex together.

Andy

I had every GI Joe they made, but I never played with any girl toys. I loved gardening. I didn't have sex for the first time till I was 20 years old. I was dating a girl and I realized that I didn't like it. Then I picked up this guy in my biology class and he fell in love with me and I just walked all over him.

Kal

I remember when my twin sister and I used to fight and the most derogatory thing she could call me was a "little faggot." So one time when I got really tired of it and I told her she would have to come up with something better than that. I walked up to the top of the staircase. My whole family was down in the living room and I screamed at the top of my lungs, "I'm A Damned Faggot. All Right. I'm A Screaming Queen. I Love...(it wasn't even true but...) I Love Big Black Dicks Shoved Up My Ass." It wasn't true at the time, but my mother fainted. She knocked over a crystal vase. It's funny because my father's Black and my mother's Irish. I have freckles and light skin. I laughed hysterically after she fainted. Then I said something really nasty to my sister that was not funny at all. I knew that she had had an abortion when she was only fourteen. I said, "At least I don't kill unborn babies. You baby killer" She hasn't called me faggot since then.

Ralph

I was attracted to this guy in high school and I was leaving on a tour so I was having a going away party. Everyone had to dress up formal, but funky, like tennis shoes with a dress. I wore shorts and a tuxedo and my friend showed up as a Chippendales guy with glitter all over his body. After the party he came back to my house. We went down to the 7-11 in his mother's Lincoln to get clove cigarettes and park. Since I was leaving I just sprung on him and grabbed him and started kissing him. We had sex in the car and we realized afterwards that the light inside the car had been on the whole time so people could see in. We killed the car battery. So, we started walking and his girlfriend saw us. We were pretty disheveled, and she picked us up. She looked at us and wondered how I got glitter all over myself.

I used to tap dance and my mother would call me Ginger. She knew. I told her after I had a bad experience with this guy who ripped us off. He wrote bad checks and my roommate got arrested trying to cash them. But she already knew. I remember because I was looking for comfort and she wasn't offering it. She thought I was crazy for getting taken.

After my sister got married, Mother didn't like any of the pictures so she didn't buy any and I asked her when we would ever be dressed up like that again for pictures. She said it would be for my wedding and I told her I would be marrying a man, and she said that I sure wouldn't be marrying a woman. She told me that she would be insulted if she wasn't invited to be a part of it. I used to dress up in my mom's old '60s dresses and smoke cigarettes. I took the car one time and went to the supermarket thinking no one would recognize me. Naturally I saw one of my teachers and she said hi. When I was 15, I went to this bar and they were having an amateur strip contest and I entered and when it came down to the finals, I saw my drama teacher in the front row cheering for me. They offered me a job dancing there but when they asked me for ID, it was all over.

Ralph

I seem to remember discovering prophylactics at age 12 or so, and when the kid next door, whom I used to jack off with (just a manly, hetero thang, mind you), left to spend a year in Switzerland, I mailed him one. It was very clumsily hidden inside a roll of film (the thought of him actually putting it on was endlessly exciting to me). This was sometime back in the last century, I hasten to add, when just thinking about something illicit was thrill enough. His mother, a nosy bitch if ever there was one, discovered it and sent it back to my mother, who probably thought it was funny, but gave me a perfunctory bawling out anyway. I retreated still farther into the closet.

Anthony

77

My mom found out I was gay when I was 17 years old. I was dating a doctor who was 32. My sister, 14, had to walk past his house to go to school. I told Mom, "I am spending the night at a woman's house." But my sister saw my car at the doctor's house and told my parents. The rumor in the neighborhood was gay people lived in the house. We lived in a town of 100,000 in Florida. My mom confronted me. "Are you gay?" she said. I said "yes." She brought in a loaded 357 magnum of my father's into my room. She screamed at me, "You have ruined your life, you're the only boy in the family, you have messed up everything and you need a shrink." I said, "No, I don't and I know what I want. I like guys." She was handing me the gun and saying, "Just shoot yourself now, you might as well, you have ruined your life, you're a mess." I ran out of the house and stayed away for four days and when I got back she was still crying. It was a strict Catholic family. Then after 30 days, she went to gay bars with me and got drunk. Then she did pot with me. Six months later my only sister came out as a lesbian and my mom did crystal and got tweaked out of her mind. Now she lives in Santa Fe.

Steve

By the time I was ten I knew I was interested in my stepfather's nude body. He liked to wander around his bedroom and out to the kitchen for a beer in just his T-shirt. He was also a foul mouthed drunk and I hated him. He had a very nice slender body though: nice ass, big arms, uncut, large when soft, didn't get much bigger when hard, and big low hanging balls. At about ten years old I found out that by adjusting his window shade I could watch him undress and he would wander around the room and stand, read his mail, and fiddle with stuff on his desk across from the window. Sometimes he would stand rubbing his ass, fingering his hole or pulling on his big balls for three or four minutes at a time. Sometimes he would pull the shade lower and the next day I would go and fix it again. I watched him have sex with my mother. I always hated her. I wonder sometimes if he put on a show for me because once he caught me at the bathroom window watching him take a bath. He asked me if I ever watched my mother and I told him no. He never told my mother. Forty years later he's still my favorite jack off fantasy.

Mike

For Halloween, my mom took us to the ten cent store and my friends were all going as hobos and devils and I was, well...I wanted to be a witch. I had three older brothers and I would wear my witch's outfit weeks before Halloween. I would run through the house with my broom between my legs and my brother would scream, "Get him out of here." My brother, who was 18, was with his girlfriend at the house and he wanted to make a good impression. So my mom took me upstairs and said, "No witches before Halloween." I have two gay brothers, but the brother who was yelling was definitely not one of them.

Sidney

Mom should have known I was gay when I...? Let me see. At eight, I loved playing with my sister's Barbie and Ken dolls. I would have my GI Joe break into their "dream house," tie Barbie up in the kitchen, and rape Ken in the master bedroom. It was quite frustrating for me that neither Ken nor GI Joe were anatomically correct. Also, I got the Barbie swimming pool set where you build the pool and I loved to build all those sets for Barbie. I taught my sister to curl Barbie's hair because she couldn't do it. At nine, I asked for the bionic woman doll, and not the bionic man, and I got it. My parents were too busy to notice me, but if they would have noticed the clues were all over the place. I played with my sister's Easy-Bake Oven and Magic-Hair Barbie. There's no baggage there. I've dealt with my parents rejection and lack of attention. I've accepted myself dammit. But they could have noticed if they would have looked.

Recently, I went with a friend across country on TWA and we always take a Barbie everywhere we'd go. So Barbie was sitting on the seat next to us and all the male flight attendants where buzzing around and ogling Barbie. We went to the bathroom and when we came back Barbie was gone but there was a note that said, "I've been upgraded to first class, darlings." So we went up to first class and there she was sitting in her own first class seat with pillows around her and a drink. She was very stylish. Anyway we all got to sit in first class that trip, all because of Barbie.

Jeff

When I was eight years old, my two uncles were 16 and 17. I begged them, "I will help you do the dishes, if you let me suck your dick." What a deal for them! One night after having sex with them many times (my father was 24 he had me at 15) I asked my uncle to screw me. He said no, but I begged him, finally he agreed but it hurt and I screamed and my dad caught us and he beat my uncle up. After that incident I had no more sex with them. That was the most depressing part of my childhood.

Later on, in high school, there was Patrick, a Cuban boy in the

8th grade. We would cut up...we were monkeys and were sent to the office; we skipped the office and went to the bathroom and played with each other in the bathroom. Also, I lived near a camping area and I played doctor with two guys. Their dads were doctors. We played games. One was a dream, an older guy had been molesting him, so he showed us what to do. One day we were in the garage. Mom was shopping. But Mom came home and we were playing around, at 16, we were nude. We were caught, she knew something was up since we were quickly trying to put our clothes back on. My mom would not let us play together anymore.

Steve

My mom is a dyke and she used to have these huge dyke garage sales when I was young, 15, with all these huge dykes and I was embarrassed by what the neighbors would think. One was a 5' 2", a bright, alcoholic, psychologist and she used to get violent with my mother. My brother had to throw her out of the house one time. I was always upset about the dykes and the garage sales and the neighbors and my mom would say, "Those who fight it the most usually are." Meaning those who fight gay things the most usually are gay. I went crazy and fought with her and was upset. I left and drove my Vespa and drove and drove. I was only 15.

Then at 18, I told her I was gay, as she was writing at her desk, and she did not look up or anything she just said, "Oh that's nice," and went on writing.

Billy

At eight, all the girls in the neighborhood and I used to play Charlie's Angels. I had to be Jill or I would not play. I mean we all had bikes and mine was red but I did not care because Jill's car was white. I still had to play Jill. Today, I have a white convertible, see how things come around. Then there is the story of when my grandma dressed me up in pearls and sent me to get the mail. I was four.

Lyle

I grew up with three sisters and parents from the old country, Italy and Spain. They are really very protective. They do not trust anybody. "This is crazy America," they said, "and even worse we are in California." So my upbringing was Edwardian, we had to dress for dinner. My older sister got me a Charlie McCarthy puppet at nine, my mother said, "What are you doing with a doll?" I said, "It's not a doll, Mom, it's a puppet." My mom yelled, "It's a doll, it's a doll, it's a doll." Then I said with the innocence and truth of a nine-year-old child, "It's not a doll, Mom, it's my boyfriend." This blew my mother away. They, my mom and dad, tried to take away the doll, my puppet, my boyfriend several times and I found it. I had the doll for years. At 13, I went on vacation; when I got home, I asked where my doll was and my sister said, "I murdered him." She showed me the remains; she lit it on fire. He was melted and I cried and buried him.

Giovanni

Recently, my parents told their friends while on a holiday in the mountains that I was gay. My mom loves to tell everyone. I think it's cathartic for her. It helps her deal with the knowledge that I am gay. So we were on holiday on the Lake of the Ozarks, Missouri. The friends had a young son, eight years old. During dinner he looked at his mother and said, "I do not want to grow up and have to marry a girl." He had heard nothing of my being gay. Well, everyone just looked at each other in surprise.

Mike

At 16, I was a switch board operator for the local newspaper in Sioux Falls, South Dakota. My job was to take complaints about the paper boys throwing the paper on the roof and on the snow banks etc. So there was this book with everyone's name and phone number in it put out by the chamber of commerce of this small city, and I had extra time so I started calling the single people. Trying to sound like a girl, I'd whisper, "Hi, do you want to have sex with me?" I used the name Bobby and once I looked up this guy who was named John Marcus

Hightly. I figured that anyone who has their middle name listed would have sex with a guy. So we talked and he was turned on and he said, "Come On Over," and I said, "but I'm a guy," and he said, "Come on over anyway!" So I rode my bike to get there, he lived in a high-security building, and I thought I was going to be shot at any second because I was going after straight guys in this conservative town. Well, he answered the door and was gorgeous. He was a Levi Strauss salesman and he a had a round bed in his living room. I still fantasize about him. Then he moved to a Victorian house and the round bed was still in the living room. Later I found out that he had sex with everyone in the city—girls and guys. This one girl got crabs from him, she's a lesbian now. I had sex with him all through college, that's eight years. He was bi and I'd call up and say, "Are you in the mood." He had the biggest dick and I did pot with him for the first time. I blew all the water out of his bong, all over him and onto the round bed. I always said, "John this is Tom, are you in the mood?" and he'd say "No, I'm not in the mood" or "come right over."

Tom

I used to do the Jane Fonda Workout Challenge and I had to tell my parents it was for conditioning for the swim team. I was 17 at the time.

Dennis

I was playing with my sister. She had a doll with a big head with long hair for makeup and stuff and I was teaching them how to do it, to put the makeup on and do the hair. I grew up in Mexico with a Mexican father, a very macho culture. My father, when he came home and saw what I was doing, was very very angry and spanked me and put me in my room. So I locked myself in the closet. Hours later they found me and I was breast feeding a doll with my shirt off in the closet and my dad went ballistic. It's something like from the frying pan into the fire; I flamed.

Mario

I got the girls and boys on the block all together to do *West Side Story*. I had them do the number, "I like to be in America." I made all the girls play the boys and all the boys play the girls. This is true. Can you believe it? I was eight or nine. My mom never cut my hair, so everyone thought I was a girl. They were rednecks. I made them lip-synch because they had no talent. I could not let them sing. I stole my mom's clothes for the production. She was not pleased. My mom told me I was gay at 13, and she got me a fake ID at 14. Somehow I worked my way into the gay club and I did a drag show, but they found out I was only 14 and kicked me out. But I think the real reason was that the other drag queens were jealous of my talent.

Terrance

I was not meeting girls, living very alone, looking at boys, I was having these feelings and yearnings and desires at a very young age. I was looking at boys even at ten years old. I'm French, from the country. At school I had a crush on the young sports teacher. I thought about him a lot and I bought gym magazines and athletic magazines and hid them. This was 30 years ago.

Pierre

When I was very young, I played with Barbie. I took GI Joe and Ken and put them together and I got in trouble for that. I remember when my sister, who was close to my age, got a Barbie doll and I got a GI Joe. I liked playing with her Barbie better than my GI Joe. That was a dead giveaway. After puberty, I spent too much time in the tent with my best friend. Mom said, "What do you do all night together?" Mom guess what?

I came out to my mother at 17. My dad was dead. My mother's very liberal. I think she always knew. I told her I was gay and she said, "like Uncle John," and I said "Uh-huh" and she said, "Oh." Then she sent me to a gay shrink, I went and I seduced the psychologist, he was 40. He called my mom and said, "Your son's fine, he is gay."

George

84

At age six, I had a major crush on the guy across the street. I told my parents that I was in love with this guy. My mom said, "No, you are not in love with him, only homosexuals are in love with other men." So I figured I was one of those and I looked it up in the dictionary. I was very logical.

Jay

I had this best friend, I was probably about eight and as you can see I like blonds (this is my blond friend). This boy was blond too and at eight we used to go swimming at the high school pool, just down the street. After two days of swimming with him I saw he could not swim well. So I taught him how to swim. I thought he was really cute. I was holding him up with my arms in the water. I kind of had my hand right there at his crotch. He looked at me and smiled and so I put my hand in his trunks. It went from there. But it didn't go far 'cause we didn't know what we were doing. He's straight now. I moved away. We were in the garage and my mother did walk in one night, while we were playing with each other. She was speechless. She yelled and we stopped. He still spent the night.

Wayne

I suppose the earrings and high heels story is my best one. I discovered Mother's jewelry box and high heels. My father was always away. I was playing with my sister's Barbies, watching Wizard of Oz without knowing how campy it was, and wanting, but not getting, an Easy-Bake Oven. I got a train set instead. That was my childhood. I was sexually active as a kid, hiding in the closet with friends. I came out at 18. I went to Europe and a lot of guys were hitting on me, at ice cream parlors in Germany and McDonald's in Amsterdam. I was terrified because my friends were straight. The rest is history. After being hit on a few times, I decided to try it. I've been out ten years now. I'm a designer, lighting, and interiors. I live in West Hollywood.

Lew

I had a vacuum cleaner fetish as a child. We had a maid and every two weeks she came and I followed her around vacuuming behind her with a toy one. I wanted a real one but my mother got me a Suzi Homemaker Oven instead. The outcome is odd. I didn't want a Suzi Homemaker Easy-Bake Oven; I wanted a vacuum cleaner.

I couldn't say "p" as a kid, so I would say "f" instead, like "flug" instead of "plug." I said, "flug it in, flug it in." My oldest brother started calling me a lesbian when I turned 11 or 12 and he was 17; he was lesbian aware. I didn't know what it meant, so it didn't hurt.

Ulysses

I was four years old. I used to want long hair, so I used toilet paper as a wig. My parents never caught me. I was fighting with the nuns at school. Always getting in trouble. I'm Italian. I would hold onto the nuns with my hands and run around the nursery.

Gene

Probably my story is when, at age two and a half, I ruined my mom's two best pairs of high heels because I was walking around with them for an afternoon. She couldn't keep me out of her closet. I stretched out the toes. Also, a clue was when I used to take the old curtains to make dresses at age ten or 11. Now I'm in the Marine Corp and play in the band—the clarinet. Don't ask, Don't Tell.

Allen

I found out my father was gay, here's an interesting twist, when I found my gay porno magazines under his bed. This is true. It took him longer to accept the fact that he was gay than me. Today we are both gay and happy about it. Mom accepts things as they are. She didn't try to kill herself or anything.

Jason

My mom asked me if I understood what gay was at the time of the 1960s protest songs. We were listening to this song, about a guy carrying a purse, trying to get out of the army. Mom said, "Do you know what that was about?" I was 18, from a family of five boys, three of whom are gay. I said, "Yes, I know that." Mom's fine with the fact that I am gay; I mean what choice does she have. She has grandchildren so she's okay. She loves and adores her gay sons. Dad's a 1950s Baptist minister. I've been a minister in MCC for 17 years and that's been real difficult for Dad. All three gay sons are leaders in gay churches, but the two straight sons are atheists and agnostics. It's taken years but now Dad is coming around. He said once, "I don't approve," and I said, "I don't need your approval for anything."

Doug

My dad found pages were being ripped out of his copies of *Playboy* and *Penthouse*. One day my mom found them all in my room and they were all of men. Now that was a big indicator. I was 13. She freaked out. She took me to church a lot more often after that and I had to go through confession and catechism to be confirmed. I survived the Catholic church.

Felix

During my younger years, from seventh to ninth grade, I lived outside of Fresno, California. It was a small farming community, in the foothills, where there was nothing to do, plain and simple, but I had a beautiful time with friends. We loved to go swimming. We would get together every Friday and Saturday night. There was Shane, Brian, Victor, Miguel, Steve, Carlos, and all the rest, everyone did something sexual with everyone else.

Carlos had a barn near the river. It was 105 degrees, even in the evening it was hot. After swimming, wearing wet jeans shorts, no underwear, we started fooling around...grabbing, touching. Carlos was the best kisser, he was part French. It all started with me and Carlos. We had oral sex and the full shebang.

My dad was a gardener and sometimes people would give him *Playboy* magazines and sometimes there was a gay magazine in the pile, amazingly. I had stacks of these magazines and I would sell them to Carlos at 25 cents each.

One day we walked to Brian's house and caught him and Shane together. We heard noises in the bedroom. And caught them in the act. Later, Shane brought up the idea of us doing a four-way. We put bales of hay on the barn floor, then we would go back and jump in the creek. Carlos and I were caught one night in the backyard in the sleeping bag. My mom was in the hospital, and Dad was with her. We thought that all our sisters were far away, but we looked up and there was Carlos' two sisters and a friend standing over us as we were having sex in the sleeping bag. They threatened us and said they were going to tell unless, "you show us what you did." They took us

to the shed and laid out the sleeping bag and turned on the light, and made us do it. The girls were 18 years old. It was humiliating. Carlos' father found out and he told my parents to keep us apart. He threatened to set Carlos' private parts on fire with gasoline. He was a very violent man. The growing up years, the gay version of the wonder years.

Francisco

My dad and my cousin and I were driving to the pool; I was seven and neither of them had shoes on and I saw the hair on their feet and toes. I said, "Dad, I don't want to grow up and be a man and have hair on my toes." He looked at me perplexed in a quandary. That was a clue.

Jack

I sang "Che Sera Sera" at my grandmother's 80th birthday party, I knew all the words at seven years old. All the relatives and friends were giving her gifts, and saying poems, and so I stood up on the piano bench and sang the whole thing by heart and people clapped and screamed. It was my triumphant debut, and my relatives were amazed that I knew the whole thing. I was Doris Day.

Nick

Me and my cousins, put towels on our heads and pretended we were the Seleka Sisters; that's the name we made up. I was eight; one cousin was gay and the other was his sister. We had a lot of fun as the Seleka Sisters.

In eighth grade, we had to do a group audio/video project. My group had the idea of a fake news program. And we had this character that was a blonde bimbo woman. Since our group was all guys, I volunteered to dress as the bimbo and acted up a storm. We videotaped it. Then presented it to our classmates. They did not know who the blonde bimbo was. They couldn't believe it when I told them she was me. It was hilarious and we got an A.

Lloyd

In high school, I was in drama. I went through the closet at home with my friend Laura. She was in drama also. We were 14 and we did this whole drag number. I thought we were great. So we showed my mother. She was just horrified. She got stone quiet! I never got punished. She made it clear though that it was not something that she liked me doing. She confiscated my Easy-Bake Oven as punishment. No, I'm joking about that part. I wouldn't have given up the Easy-Bake Oven. I would have put on that dress and walked out of the house and ran away.

Henry

I didn't have a girlfriend by age 18. I never hung out with girls and my mom was real suspicious. Eventually my friends were a give-away. They were a bit queenie. I had one friend named Jerry and I said, "When you meet my mom don't say much 'cause you are a screamer and I don't want her suspecting that I am gay." I was only 18. So, when he came to the house he was very quiet and behaved, butching it up very well. But when he saw the curtains, he blurted out to my mom, "Those curtains don't go with that flower arrangement." That was a big oops.

Kyle

When I was only five I wanted to stay up late and watch Miss America. My father agreed because he thought it was to watch the girls. He thought I was a budding straight, but I said, "No Dad, I don't want to watch the girls, I want to watch it for the dresses." This he could not understand.

Glen

Years ago, my baby-sitter had a boyfriend who would come over and hang around in his underwear. I was obsessed with the boyfriend's underwear whenever he stayed over. I went into the bathroom and looked at it when he took them off. It got me excited, it was a fancy brand. I was 12 years old.

90

When I lived in Michigan, I was in sixth or seventh grade and there was this one kid who reached puberty before everyone else. He had really hairy legs and he was in my gym class and I used to fantasize that I could have an orgy with him.

When I was in the play *Peter Pan*, in sixth grade, I wanted to be Peter so I could wear the stockings, but they made me be the father.

Between ten and 12, my brothers bought Jockey underwear and I would cut out the little cute models from the photo on the package and hide them. But my brother found them so I burned the rest. He stole some of them and kept them, so I guessed he was gay too.

In Arizona at 14, as a freshman in high school, I loved to have a full body tan. I sunbathed nude in the back yard, so when I had to take a shower at gym class I would look good for all the other boys.

When I was about to turn 18, I counted down the days until I could go to a porno bookshop and buy magazines. I went in there on my birthday and bought five or six gay ones. I hid them at home under my desk drawer, but they fell out and my sister found them. She told my mom eventually. But first she was asking weird questions like, "Don't you want to have kids?" trying to figure if I was gay or not. I said that I do not want kids. She said that I wasn't going to find a girl who doesn't want kids. "Yes I will. I know one right now." Later my mom came and said, "your sister found these mags in your room while she was looking for magic markers." I totally freaked out and I said that I bought them for my friend Lori. I didn't care, I was stressed out. They should have figured it out.

Finally, my mom just came out and asked me if I was gay and I said, "What if I said I was?" And she said she wouldn't love me and I was totally shaking. Throughout that time, she told me to stay away from Camel Back. That is where the gay clubs are. And I thought "Oh, is that where the gay clubs are?" She said "weird people are there, and gays are there and I don't want you around them." So I headed right over to Camel Back to a bookstore and that is where and how I first met someone.

Reid

When I was six years old, we used to play sex games, like touch my willy. That started it all but then I wanted to have sex with an older man. I didn't at that age, but when I was about 13, I did have sex with a 15 year old. I am Asian and from Amsterdam. My mom had sisters and they used to love to dress me up as a girl. They did it to me, but I wasn't interested in drag. Never have been. When I was 22 years old, I wanted a doll, not a car, not a little doll either. I wanted a big huge one. Also, I wanted a Jeep just like my father's. I got a big doll and I named it Margie. One time when I went out on the street my father caught me out there dressed up like a girl. That caused a few problems for me and the family even in Amsterdam.

At a birthday party I did an Indonesian dance and it is even on video tape. My father was very embarrassed, because I looked like a little girl.

I saw a David Bowie picture when I was like 16 in a Bowie interview in a magazine. And the quotation said, "David Bowie admits he's bisexual," and I had to look up the word and then I knew immediately that that was what I was. And so from that moment on Bowie was my hero. I bought the magazine and hid the magazine just for that sentence.

At nine, I went swimming with two older girls. There were two pools next to each other at that time in Amsterdam, one was for boys and one was for girls. So the girls said come with us. And of course it wouldn't have been a problem, if one little boy was in the girls pool especially at my age. But the girls made me dress up in a two-piece bathing suit with a swim cap and then they made me go up to and ask the lifeguard what time it was. This was all to prove I was acting like a girl.

Kal

My mother caught me wearing my sister's dress. So she made me wear it all day long as punishment. And then hours later in the day she caught me having fun in the dress, flinging it around and swaying and dancing. She said that I shouldn't have fun in the dress and made me take it off.

Stacey

At eight, I watched *The Sound of Music*, with Eva Gardener, right? She wore a ball gown with evening gloves to the elbow. I told my Mom that they looked really beautiful and that I wanted a pair just like them. She said you can't have those because they are women's gloves. Mothers are not always right.

David

At age seven, the first tip-off that I can remember was when I got in the shower with a friend of mine. And my mom came in. I guess that little boys shower together, but my mom was somehow aware that it wasn't okay. That this wasn't kosher. She didn't do anything, she just scolded us. Also, I had a Big Jim doll and a Big Jack and Big Josh and a Winnabago for going camping. I loved to play and there were no girls ever on my camping trips, period. I was into Big Jim from ages seven-13.

Doug

My gay story is that when I was four years old, the only toy that I wanted for Christmas was a set of dishes, play dishes, and my mom got them for me! My parents are very conservative. I have it all on video. In kindergarten, I was fixated and infatuated with another boy and I followed him around. At three, I looked for grandmother's pumps when I came over and I wore them the whole time I was there and they let me, because I threw a fit if they didn't.

Brad

At four, I packed up all my mom's makeup in her purse and went door to door trying to sell it to the neighbor ladies. I had handiwipes to take the makeup off my face after each demonstration and reapply at the next house. I was the youngest Avon lady ever. At 16, I dressed in drag every day while my parents were in Europe and I sat in the house drinking tea with my legs crossed. Now I am a body builder and very athletic and work in accounting. I'm very masculine. Really. No really.

Walter

I somehow knew that I couldn't have or ask for a Barbie doll, but I had to get myself a girl doll so I hatched this plan. I asked my father to get me the *Star Wars* Luke Skywalker Doll—a butch male doll. I then said I was starting a collection of *Star Wars* dolls. And asked for a Princess Lea doll. At 12, I wanted a Princess Lea doll, so I had to start a whole collection.

Michael

My brother dressed me in a wig and makeup and he did a dragfest with me at six years old: a performance with pictures for the whole family. I have the pictures but I have never done drag since. Later, I was totally in love with this guy who was a twin. I always talked about him and wanted him to go on vacation with my family. That should have been a clue.

Nelson

Once, my mom caught me doing something sexual; I was wearing her silk house robe and I had a hard-on and I was nine or ten years old. I was in front of a mirror doing it too. She was a little taken aback by the sight, let me tell you. Then I was caught sewing my own shirt from a sewing pattern...that was the second clue that I was gay. In fact, my dad called me a girl then. I was 12. Mom thought it was neat. I was too religious to do anything too bad.

Scott

She figured it out I think because I was having friends over all the time, all through my childhood, starting at nine or ten. She wondered why I constantly had the kids staying over night with me. I knew when I was nine or ten that I was gay. I always had boys around me and I knew I did not like girls. I played a lot of doctor. The first time I knew I liked it with boys was when my stepbrother and I got into bed and he played with me and I loved it. He screwed me, that triggered something, it hurt me, but I loved it. After that, I couldn't get enough of it. I never dressed in girls' clothes. All I wanted to do was be around guys. Mom knew something was wrong, she found out the sheets were wet in the morning, but she never asked me about it. She always asked, "Bob, where are your girlfriends?"

Bob

I was ten when Mom found my love letters to Andrew and Chuck and Glenn. She was looking through my drawers and at the bottom of the underwear drawer she found them and they were as graphic as a ten year old could be about sex. Also, I had taken a pair of my sister's bikini thongs, and was wearing them backwards to cover my genitals. When my sister found herself missing one of her bikinis, all my mother said was, "Don't wear your sister's clothes." When I was 11, I had gone to a gay beach but I didn't know it. I just saw all these beautiful stylish men on the beach in these skimpy speedo bathing suits and I wanted to be like that, and that is why I stole my sister's bikini.

Harry

My mother had the most beautiful long nightgown, and I loved to get into that thing. And she had a pastel orchid lotus blossom thing that went over it. And I would run around the house with it flowing behind me. It's so weird because my parents were straight and conservative and I wore all my mother's clothes. And they didn't mind. They must have read Dr. Spock or something.

George

When I was playing doctor with a girl next door, I put Tide detergent in her pussy because it smelled so bad. She never played doctor with me again. And in Boy Scouts everyone played around with everyone. That is why I think it is such a joke about gays in the Boy Scouts controversy, everyone fooled around in that organization; it was a right of passage.

Leo

When I was 14 years old, I was into photography and I had my own darkroom and I had no idea that I was gay. I am sure that my mom did not suspect. I would take pictures of the body-building contests on television because I couldn't buy body-building magazines or anything. I would keep the pictures I had developed behind my bed. Eventually Mom found them and she was mystified—all of these male body-builder photos from the blurry TV screen.

Roger

When I was four years old, I enjoyed going to my parents' country club. Every time the lifeguard had to use the bathroom, I jumped up and followed him in. A few times my father caught me just sitting there in the locker room on the bench swinging my legs and watching him take a shower. I outed myself at 15 when I was coming out of anesthesia from having my wisdom teeth removed and I was crying and saying, "I am sorry I am gay, Dad, I am sorry I'm gay." That was the only time my dad held me when I cried and I don't remember it.

Clark

Speak to my friend Marilyn. She has a grandson that's...We know he's gay in the making. You see his mom took him to Target to buy new shoes and his mom made the mistake of saying, "You can have any pair you want." So, of course, they walked by the girls shoes first and the little boy saw these bright plastic sandals with colored jewels and he wanted those. He threw a fit in the store when she tried to get him away from that section. So Mom just bought some plain boys shoes and left. They got home and after awhile Mom showed the box to the boy. He picked up the shoes and walked to the trash can and threw them away without saying a word. Days later at the grandmother's house, Mom asked about the new shoes. He glared, stomped off and he came back a few minutes later wearing grandma's Gold metallic pumps and bracelets and said "All pretty now." You could write a whole book about that kid alone.

Kent

My Mom should have known I was gay at age seven or eight. During a family gathering, I lip-synched a Julie Andrews album (I think it was *The Sound of Music*, but it could have been, *Mary Poppins*) as a lullaby for my younger brothers. When the two of them had fallen asleep, I had plenty more of the album side left, so I lip-synch-lullabied our family dog to sleep as well.

Kerry

My parents should have know I was gay when I wanted a Miss America Doll when I was about six years old! They got me the doll and I would change the clothes, etc. But I could tell that my grandfather was not happy with me playing with it at all. At 11 years old, I had my entire closet organized by color, size and style and would proudly show my family and friends. They should have known, how could they not?

Felix

I went on a 4WD, family, bush weekend with my family. I live in Australia and am an Aussie, and we went with my best friend who lived two doors down the road. I shared the tent with him and another friend. One night when we were getting ready to go to bed and getting undressed in the tent. I quickly pulled out my camera and started taking photos of my friend in his Y front underwear, and teasing him that I would put them on public display. Well, I was excited after all, I knew he had a good tanned bod' and was well hung. To see photos of all this would be the ultimate and all at my disposal. A few weeks later, back home my father came into my room one night and sat me down and started asking me some strange questions. (Of which, I can only remember the feeling of, "Oh, he has to know but how?") He ended up handing me the photos of my friend and asked me to explain why they existed. I told him we were having fun, (as guys do when camping) and said I would give them to him when I saw him in school. Strange thing was my friend never saw them and never got the pictures back from me and my dad never knew how close he was to uncovering a deep secret. All I can say is the photos provided many moments of enjoyment and eventually ended up being traded in for the real thing 12 months later, much to my enjoyment! And I think to his enjoyment too. True story.

Todd

When I was 18, I was living in Fresno, and I heard the Village People sing that song "YMCA." It sounded so fun. I told my parents that I wanted to go to San Francisco for my 18th birthday and stay at the YMCA. I had never been on an airplane before. I stayed at the YMCA and it was awful, dirty and horrible, if you know it. But years later I found Laguna Beach and thought I had found Heaven.

Colin

I remember one year, I asked for a doll for Christmas. I think that would be a give-away. I was like four years old. I got it. It was a baby doll in a crib. My sister used to dress me up as a little girl and parade me around at five. She introduced me as cousin Debbie. I remember my mother gave away the clothes and I was so mad. So was my sister.

Kevin

I was 13 years old. There was this guy Marty Flechers, who was 18; he helped the gym teacher and he changed with us before first-period gym class. He had the most beautiful, perfect muscled body and I looked at it and said I want to have a body like that someday. I was 13 at the time. I wonder what he looks like now. I hope he has kept his body. Today I work out and I have a pretty good body. Once, when I was 13, at school all the girls were talking about Jean Claude Van Damme. How great he was. I chimed in, "Yeah, he's really cute." They just looked at me with a look like—"do you realize what you just said?"—a really strange look. Maybe I should have known then that something was up.

Bobby

Mom should have known and I should have known it too. Questions about whether I was gay probably started over the fights we had at home over whether the family was going to watch Bonanza or Judy Garland! On Sunday night in 1963, it was CBS vs. NBC, Bonanza in color vs. Judy Garland in black and white. I lost. Back then my family was too powerful, but after I was on my own I got to listen to Judy as often as I wanted. I'm still watching her and listening to her every day. Back then, at home, we settled it by getting a second small TV. I was ten.

Also, I had an inordinate interest in my mother's handbags that she thought was strange. She wanted me shopping in the sporting goods section. Spending time in the handbag department against my mother's wishes has lead to a career in retail. I never wanted to dress like her though.

At 18, the most embarrassing moment of my life occurred. There was an invention called a jack-pack. I don't know if it's still around. This sewed things up for me being gay. It was inflatable and the shape of a football, something that you penetrated. The magazine ad for this thing had a picture. I cut out the picture and coupon order form. Somehow the coupon got stuck to my breakfast plate and she found it stuck there. That was a real give away. I got one eventually and used it in college.

Timothy

When I was seven or eight, I had this big crush on the guy across the street. I always felt I wanted to be near him and sit by him. Since my family was the only one with a TV on the block, he came over a lot. It wasn't sexual. It was just the need to be next to someone of the same sex. Like all kids, we messed around sexually with each other. The whole block was kids having sex. But two of us in particular always ended up doing a lot more than the rest. I was born in Cuba. This all happened in Castro's Cuba. The other guys and I when we had sex used the excuse that we were doing it to practice.

Tommy

I was born and raised in Trinidad and Tobago, remote twin islands in the Caribbean. I have come to the conclusion that all gay folk have shared experiences as children growing up. We knew that we were different. There's always gossip at the gay clubs and bars about drag queens and their big attitudes, not to mention the hairdos. Well, I will tell you one thing, I worked those runways when I was only four years old. When I reflect on my childhood, anyone who did not know that I was gay had to be a fool, especially my parents. I recall staging a Miss Universe pageant with my three older sisters. You don't even have to guess who won! I got into my youngest sisters bikini, tucked my dick between my legs, put on my mom's pumps, stuffed the bra to look like Dolly Parton and the next thing I knew, I was Miss Universe and the world was never the same.

As a child I attended many wedding ceremonies with my parents at the age of six, I decided it was time I had my own. Having an East Indian background, all the ethnic weddings are long and tedious. Three days to be exact. One Sunday, I gathered together my sisters and girl cousins, of which I had many. There would have been havoc if I wasn't chosen to be the blushing bride! The one thing embedded in my mind about this event is that I was also a fashion icon at the time. For the veil I took lace curtains that my mom had; at one end I folded it fan-like, creating a sort of crown for the head piece. What an effect. Eat this Calvin Klein.

All went well with the ceremony and after the reception, Peter, the groom, and I zoomed off into the sunset in our Mercedes Convertible (actually a skateboard). The night of the honeymoon is another story altogether.

Playing hopscotch and doll house with the girls was a regular activity. However, another event during childhood that took a grand prize was the day I decided to have a full make-over and become the real me with makeup.

My mother left the house as usual for work and I began applying carefully the foundation my mom used. Then I proceeded to put her blush on my cheeks, the ones on my face. Not forgetting the eyeliner and the mascara, the Chinese red lipstick and gloss was left for last. As the make-over was complete, I decided to finish the look by getting into one of my sister's frilly dresses and shoes and carrying my mom's purse. One has to accessorize. As I twirled in front of the full-length mirror in my mom's room, guess who walks in? Mommie Dearest—she forgot her purse!

Carlos

I knew I was gay when I felt strange when I had to take a shower with my dad, even at three years old. Soon after that, my dad forced me to move on to taking baths. My parents found out I was gay at 13 or 14 when I was in eighth grade. I had a PE, physical education, orange folder, with sports figures, pictures, sports drawings on it. I had to

have one. I was really majorly into sports. I wrote, "I love _ _ _ _ _
_ _ _ _ _." On the outside of the folder. And there were blanks for all
the letters of the guy's first and last names. I must have been really
screwed up, then I started writing, "I love Joe Montana." I was in
Wisconsin. When my parents caught me doing something else, like
smoking or drinking, I was considered to be bad, and I had to go to
Denver. I left the PE folder in Wisconsin. My parents found the
folder, but they didn't tell me; they just sent me to therapy with no
explanation. After going to the therapist for a while, he told me that
my parents wanted me to know something, that he was supposed to
bring up something. He said, "Your parents found this folder that
says, "I love baseball players," "I love men." And I told the therapist
that it was a friend's and not mine. And they all bought it.

Vernon

I used to make clothes for my GI Joe doll. I was young, maybe eight,
at the time. I created a puppet show and I rigged the sets and back-
drops between the doors. It was very extensive; I created all the costumes and put on the whole show—very theatrical. By ten, I was
doing musicals. I didn't actually wear dresses or fool around with a
guy until I was 21 years old.

Brad

At 17, I bought out an entire Banana Republic store before a safari
summer trip I took to Africa, all khaki clothes and coordinated colors.
I was a rich kid growing up, so that allowed me to indulge in these
things. I always did all the cookies and decorating at Christmas for
my mom. This began as early as three and lasted well beyond 13.
But I did butch things too, like hunting and fishing. But I began to
hate killing at 12. Eventually I cut down on the killing trips, the
hunting and fishing. At 15, I drew up all the plans for the re-land-
scaping of our house. I also created plans for a deck. I remember that
I loved Erasure, and Dead or Alive, I listened to a lot of gay groups.

Justin

103

This occurred about the age of 17. As a teenager, I bought body-builder muscle magazines. I hid them until one day my mom found them and mistook them for gay magazines and said, "What are all these men wearing no clothes in funny positions?" I guess the posing shorts were skimpy and the poses and muscles very hypermasculine. Perhaps she was looking for evidence to confirm her intuition.

Greg

Oh God, I got caught by the maid at 12, when I put my mom's white dress on. It had these nasty flowers on it and the maid came and caught me. I didn't even know that she was in the house and I heard her and I hid in the shower but she caught me and I begged her not to tell my mom. And can you guess what she did? Of course, she told my mom, and my mother told my father. I got in trouble. But not too bad. There must have been a lot of strange things I was doing.

Malcolm

I was a masseur for the football squad at 12 years old. That should have told my mom that maybe I was gay. Actually we call soccer "football" in Italy so it was really the soccer team. My mother may have guessed, but she never said anything. She never caught me fooling with a guy. But I enjoyed massaging the team. Do you have that in America? Massage boys for the team?

Skip (Translated from Italian)

I would incessantly watch *Mary Tyler Moore* with my mother, *MTM* reruns every night at age nine. Also, I was a girl frequently for Halloween, but my mother encouraged this, she would say, "Oh, be a girl again." She had no clue, she just liked seeing me happy and she knew dressing as a girl for Halloween made me happy. My sister caught me once trying on her makeup. She teased my about it and years later when I told her I was gay, she said, "I knew you were a fag the day I caught you trying on my makeup."

Claudio

At four years old, my mom said she noticed I was fascinated with her pumps. At five years old, I used to play wedding and wanted to be the bride. At ten, I kept asking my mom for the family china, that's when she should have known I was gay. I wanted that china and I didn't want it going to my sister.

Lane

My parents did know. They pulled me out of ballet at age 13 because I was becoming too effeminate. I credit my mother, she put me in ballet in the first place. The only boy in Omaha, Nebraska in the ballet class. At 29, I told her I was gay and somehow she was surprised. Today I dance in European ballet.

Tim

When I was 14, I went to my first rock concert, Duran Duran, and I screamed out the names of all the guys for two hours. Looking back, if anyone would have noticed that should have given them a clue. At 15, I went and saw Madonna in concert. I made my dad pay $250 each for the tickets for me and my sister and I bought the mesh bra and T-shirt. It was the Virgin tour.

Henry

I convinced my mother that she had to put my hair in curlers for school. I told her it was for a sports club initiation or for a joke or skit or something. So she did it for me. I went to school that way and got beat up. I don't know what kind of result I was hoping for. Now, as you can see, I'm bald.

Peter

My grandmother told me when I was 17 years old that I was gay. I was going out with this girl and I was in high school and we had a party at my house. And I was being quite over the top. I was bopping to an ABBA song doing all the hand movements and really getting into it. I was having the time of my life. The next day my grandmother, who was 65, said very matter-of-factly and certainly, "You are gay." I said "really."

She's 97 now and she keeps saying, "I knew I was right, I knew I was right. I knew he was gay." She is very loving and accepting of it. She also picked up that my father was gay, but it took him longer to come out. He was 40.

Nevin

I was a sickly kid and at nine I painted everything in rainbows. Every shirt I colored had a rainbow, every sky had a rainbow. One summer, I hiked my shorts up high so I would have no tan line. Then I dry cleaned my backpack, at age ten, and ironed my corduroy pants. I had a *Charlie's Angels'* lunch box at 11. At 12, I asked my friend to show me his penis. His was bigger, so I didn't show him mine. My

family used to vacation in the winter at warm places and I would catch myself looking at all the guys around the pool. I thought that I just wanted to be like them, but I noticed that I was looking at them a lot from ages 13-17. It's strange because a part of me noticed myself looking at guys.

Broc

I was overly creative throughout my childhood. I wanted a Ken doll or GI Joe. I was five or six years old, and what they got me was a Ken doll. I couldn't throw a ball for the life of me. I was always best at doing my sister's doll's hair at nine years old. At age ten, I was a little league disaster. Then I did Geraldine imitations from the Flip Wilson Show at 11 through 13 years old. The final straw was when my mom noticed that I got hard when I looked at the Sears catalogue men's section. She freaked out and my dad had a talk with me.

Kyle

When I was young all my friends were girls. Later, I played doctor with the boys but not the girls. I lived in a little town and I saw nothing gay at all, just ridiculous stereotypes, until the age of 15. I thought I was the only one in this world like me.

Wallace

I fell in love with Butch at 16; I used to just stare at him. Once, I made him uncomfortable because of my staring, he was sitting at lunch with his shirt off. I was skinny. He had muscles and hair on his chest. Finally he said, "what are you staring at" or something like that or he just gave me a look. He was very kind about it though.

Xavier

When I was five and six, I hung around girls. Age eight, when I dressed up in dress-up clothes, I wore the dresses and wigs. I had a Farrah Fawcett doll. My friends were girls all the way up to 20.

Billy

On my fourth birthday, I put on my mom's pumps, grabbed her purse and walked around the backyard, prancing about. And everything was pink. No matter what color anything was if you asked me I said it was pink. "What color is the sky, Kip?" "Pink," "What color is the tree?" "Pink." This was a wild episode. Also, I was really attached to my mom till I was 14.

Kip

I don't know. I didn't know myself until very late. I mean I can look back. I preferred reading over sports. I played tag with girls not kickball or softball with the boys. But I didn't know myself as a kid. Perhaps an outside observer should have noticed when I put on my mom's dress and twirled around. I got my brothers to do it too, but they were all straight. How I persuaded my straight brothers to twirl and dress in drag I will never know. I rearranged my room every six months. That was a clue when I was ten. I only cried when my redesign didn't work.

Luke

When I was 18, I went home after traveling around Europe on my own and working and swimming competitively in a private school that my parents sent me to and almost going to the Olympics. I told my parents I was gay and we didn't speak to each other for nearly a year. And when I came home again, my mother didn't believe me. She thought I was a drug addict. She looked at my arms for heroin trails. She couldn't believe it because I always had girlfriends.

I went out for the first time with a guy at school, a long weekend, my straight friends and I went to a club, The Broadway, a trendy place. They wouldn't let us in, it was too full, so we went to a gay club. I was excited but I pretended like I didn't care. We went in the club and danced. The barman was talking to me, so I sent my girlfriend to get the drinks. At 5 am, the girls left me at the club, because my bus home wasn't till 7 am, so I sat in a corner and this guy walked by and talked to me. I was cold toward him but he was persistent.

Nothing happened that night. We met the next weekend. I stole some dorm keys and snuck out to meet him every night and then hurried back to the dorm to be there at 6 am. I went three days without sleeping. I went to the infirmary to pretend I was sick, just so I could sleep.

After that I became a right-wing, punk, skin-head anti-gay, 'cause I couldn't accept myself. I went to drinking and drugs. And I quit swimming at that time. And my friends hated me. That was a year. I was thrown out of school 'cause I wasn't attending class and I slapped a teacher. The French teacher told me to take off my hat. And I said the girls can wear hats and she said it was society rules that guys can't wear hats indoors and I had to take it off. So, I slapped her and the other teachers tried to talk with me, but I couldn't even talk about my sexuality. And it was all because I was gay and couldn't accept it.

Oscar, France

The sweater story, a turtle neck ski sweater is the center of this story when I was seven. I saw this movie where they had two huge guys trapped in a cow suit. It was an Arabian night story. The villain was saying, "As the leather dries it will squeeze you tighter and tighter until your eyes will pop from your head and your tongue will hang swollen from your mouth." How bleak was my puberty that I had to watch this on TV. Anyway, this got me hot. So I decided to improvise this scene at home. It was about 1964 and I used a turtle neck sweater as the cow suit. I put my legs through the arm holes and I put my dick through the turtle neck and I hung myself from a doorknob on the closet.

We lived in a house with hardwood floors and long hallways and I was masturbating in the sweater when I was seven and I heard my mother say, "darling darling," but I could not move. I struggled wildly but I was stuck. When my mother opened the door, I was hanging there. Well, she saw me and to this day she has never said a word about it.

Ben

When I was eight years old, I remember being fascinated with a boy-friend that my older sister had. He must have been about 20. I remember sitting at the kitchen table and playing with his hair, which was very long. This was all from a boy of eight so that shows me that it was all very early. That should have been the first clue.

Later, I sucked the end of a canary water feeder when I was 15 and my mom caught me and asked me what I was doing. I was in the kitchen and I thought I was alone. Somehow the tip, the end of the water feeder, looked very interesting. And I kind of started to give it head, to suck on it, and rhythmically put it in my mouth. I guess my mom had been standing there for a minute because she finally shrieked and said, "What are you doing?" That was very embarrassing.

Mark

I told mom I was gay when I was 16 years old. She said, "I've known longer than you have." I knew at five, when I would throw a deck of cards on the floor of the locker room on purpose. Then I would pick up the cards very slowly so that I could watch the men getting dressed. I was a waterboy for the football and track team. I would rather play the piano than play sports in Junior High. I wanted a perm in second grade that's when my mom knew. I got it too. I hassled my parents until they couldn't take it anymore. Everyone made fun of me at school. I was humiliated. I was just a six-year-old queen saying, "I want curly hair, God dammit." At 13, the neighbor boy's mother came home and caught me playing doctor with her son, she sent me home and called my mother.

Otto

I used to always invite my friends over for sleep outs and the funny thing is that I am still doing the same thing. We played and I asked them if they would let me suck their dicks and they did and that is one reason why of course they kept coming over for sleepovers all the time. I was 12 to 15. I still love sleepovers. Doesn't everyone?

Ike

110

At age of seven, the high school football field was across the street from my house and I would go out in front of the entire high school marching band, as they did their formations, wearing my sister's cheerleading skirt, twirling a fire baton. They didn't do anything or try to stop me. "Oh, there's that little kid in drag twirling fire batons again." I didn't like to cut the lawn but I would use the gas from the mower to light the batons. It was Indiana, you could play with fire.

Percival

When I asked for a baby doll at age four or five for my birthday—one of those big ones one that you would normally buy a girl. That certainly was a clue that I was gay at an early age. I had a Barbie and Ken doll at six or seven. Also I was taking tap dancing lessons in first grade, Jazz in third.

Living in Ohio when I was six, I was in the bathroom and my mom was hanging her panty hose in there. So I tried them on. She came in and I was wearing her panty hose. That was a real shock and surprise. I took those things off so fast without a tear.

I wouldn't mow the grass when I was a kid unless I had showered and done my hair. It drove my father crazy.

In college I was always bringing guys home, never girls; we slept downstairs and made noises and my dad would come down to see what was going on. All my high school friends were female. Now I am a flight attendant, living in Chicago, visiting L.A.

Reid

I think my mother did know I was gay when I put on a pair of women's shoes and I got a hard-on when I was five. I knew something was wrong with me, they used to have these Johnny West dolls but I always played with the Jan West doll. I was more into the cowgirl look than the cowboy look. But in Spain little boys wear skirts so it was okay, my mother wanted me to be a girl.

Neil

Each day I would bring all my stuffed animals, I had 40 of them, in the TV room. I would make cup cakes and stuff out of playdough. I made my mother come in and join us to light candles on the birthday cakes. I was into dinner parties at an early age. I wanted an Easy-Bake Oven, but Mom would never get it for me.

Alexander

At family reunions I remember being in the middle of the room doing impersonations of Lily Tomlin as the operator, Flip Wilson as Geraldine, I was always impersonating a woman. The fact that they didn't know then is pretty funny, this was like first, second grade.

Billy

I was dressing in my sister's dress, at eight, wrapping a towel around my head. Unbeknownst to me, the air conditioner repairman was in the house. He said, "What the hell are you doing?" He looked up and said, "Oh God, I don't want to pry." I remember the dress, a nice yellow shift. I haven't done drag much since, but I have a thing for air conditioner repairmen. Just kidding.

Ron

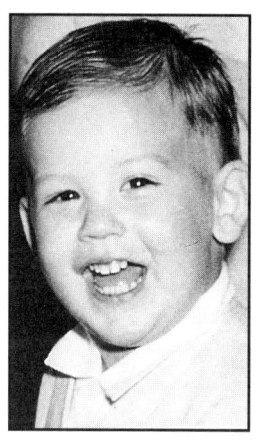

Michael Zambotti

Michael Zambotti has been an actor, dancer and a writer of screenplays. He has just completed a novel, *Prague Diaries*.

A graduate of Pennsylvania State University, Zambotti has worked for top corporations including IBM, Hewlett Packard, as well as computer animation companies. He lived as a Zen monk for a year, studying with Robert Aiken.

He has lived in Prague, Berlin, Northern Italy and Australia. Presently, he divides his time between San Diego, Los Angeles and New York. He is currently producing a motion picture. Zambotti's home page is www.execworld.net/mike/. A more recent baby picture of him can be found on the cover.

116

Frisch

Frisch is a free-lance artist best known for his cartoons of the "bear" subculture and his political cartoons appearing in San Francisco's *Bay Area Reporter*. He also draws "The Adventures of Maxx and Harley," a cartoon series appearing in *Bear* Magazine. In 1998, Frisch produced a full-color calendar of "Beartoons," he hopes will become an annual production. His "bearart" also appears on T-shirts, mugs, refrigerator magnets and all sorts of other "bearaphanalia."

Frisch grew up in St. Paul, MN and studied fine art at the University of Wisconsin. He now resides in San Francisco with his lover of eight years. (Photo by Jim Wigler.)

118

The aunts should of known after I wore their hats every year.

Frisch

Other Books

from

ALAMO SQUARE PRESS

Other Books from Alamo Square Press:

Being • Being Happy • Being Gay

Pathways to a Rewarding Life for Lesbians and Gay Men. *The make-your-life-work book* by Bert Herrman. "Herrman extends a compassionate and useful hand in the journey toward realizing our full human potential." —Mark Thompson, *The Advocate.* ISBN: 0-9624751-0-6/paper/$8.00

Hard Plays/Stiff Parts

The homoerotic plays of leading gay playwright Robert Chesley, featuring "Jerker," "Night Sweat" and "Dog Plays." ISBN: 0-9624751-1-4/paper/$9.95

In God's Image

Christian Witness to the Need for Gay/Lesbian Equality in the Eyes of the Church by (Episcopal) Fr. Robert Warren Cromey. "Nurturing, healing...a call to action."— Malcolm Boyd. ISBN: 0-9624751-2-2/paper/$9.95

Pei Yu: Boy Actress

In the final dynasty of China, the women's roles were played on the stage by young men also trained to serve the personal needs of the Chinese noblemen. This is an exquisite turn-of-the-century novel written by George Soulié de Morant, a Frenchman who lived during the period. Art Nouveau illustrations by Nemi Frost. ISBN: 0-9624751-3-0/cloth/$19.95. ISBN: 0-962741-4-9/paper/$12.95

TRUST / The Hand Book

A guide to the sensual and spiritual art of handballing by Bert Herrman. ISBN: 0-9624751-5-7/paper/$12.00

Tough Acts to Follow

One-Act Plays on the Gay/Lesbian Experience edited by Noreen Barnes and Nicholas Deutsch. ISBN: 0-9624751-6-5/paper/$9.95

Out of the Bishop's Closet

The Daring Testimony of Faith of a Gay Mormon High Priest by Antonio A. Feliz. Fleeing the tyranny of the Church, Feliz escapes with secrets that would make Brigham Young turn pale. ISBN: 0-9624751-7-3/paper/$12.95

We Oughta Be in Pictures...

Two hilarious lesbian screenplays by Julia Willis and a history of lesbians in the cinema. ISBN: 0-9624751-8-1/paper/$9.95

What the Bible *Really* Says About Homosexuality

Recent findings by top scholars offer a radical new view. The long-awaited, mind-expanding bestseller by Daniel A. Helminiak, Ph.D., a Roman Catholic Priest and respected theologian. ISBN: 0-9624751-9-X/paper/$9.95

Gay Tales of the Samurai

Three-hundred-year-old stories of male/male love in feudal Japan based on historical accounts by Ihara Saikaku, translated by E. Powys Mathers. ISBN: 1-886360-00-6/paper/$9.95

Lavender Reflections

Affirmations for lesbians and gay men by Eleanor Ruth Wagner with vital quotations and photographs by Victor Arimondi. "A marvelous addition to the growing library of books on affirmation"—*Lavender Lifestyle*. ISBN: 1-886360-02-2/paper/$10.95.

Sundays at Seven

An anthology of works by Los Angeles gay writers who took part in A Different Light's gay writer's series in the '70s and '80s. Includes work by Paul Monette, Mark Thompson, Bernard Cooper, Michael Nava and others. Edited by Rondo Mieczkowski ISBN: 1-886360-01-4/paper/$12.00.

Stars Without Garters!

The memoirs of two gay GI's in WWII by C. Tyler Carpenter & Edward H. Yeatts; with photos. ISBN: 1-886360-03-0/cloth/$20.00. ISBN: 1-886360-04-9/paper/ $12.00.

Two Flutes Playing

A Spiritual Journeybook for Gay Men by Andrew Ramer. ISBN: 1-886360-95-7/ paper/$12.95

To purchase copies of these books, send a check or money order for the price of each book requested plus $2.00 for the first book and $.50 for each additional book (for postage and handling) to:

Alamo Square Distributors
P.O. Box 14543
San Francisco, CA 94114

Outside of the United States, money must be sent in U.S. currency. There is no additional cost for shipping to Canada, but readers from all other countries must send $5.00 per title (for air-mail postage and handling).

Alamo Square Press is an affiliate of Alamo Square Distributors. Please write or call for a full catalogue of books for gay men and lesbians from over a hundred publishers. Also available are catalogues of books on "Cross-dressing and Gender Dysphoria," and "SM/Leather/Fetish."